More French You Use Without Knowing It

More Stories
of
Fascinating Words

by

Saul H. Rosenthal

More French You Use Without Knowing It

More Stories of Fascinating Words

Published by Wheatmark®
610 East Delano Street, Suite 104, Tucson, Arizona 85705 U.S.A.
www.wheatmark.com

ISBN: 978-1-60494-524-9
LCCN: 2010937289

Books in this Series
by Saul H. Rosenthal

The Rules for **the Gender of French Nouns**, (3rd revised edition)

Speaking Better French, **Faux Amis**

Speaking Better French, **more Faux Amis**

Speaking Better French, **still more Faux Amis**

French Faux Amis: The Combined Book

Speaking Better French, **The Key Words and Expressions**

Speaking Better French, **More Key Words and Expressions**

French Key Words and Expressions: The Combined Book

All the French You Use Without Knowing It
More French You Use Without Knowing It

et en français

Les règles du genre des noms *au masculin et au féminin*

Mieux parler anglais, ***Faux amis***

Appreciations

I must begin by thanking Catherine Ostrow again. In spite of her teaching duties, Catherine again eagerly volunteered to read the entire manuscript of this book. She made many helpful corrections of errors I would never have caught myself, made excellent suggestions, and gave me lots of encouragement

I also wish to thank my daughter Sadie who kindly also read the entire manuscript and made many useful suggestions and corrections. Her younger eyes caught errors I had looked right past, and her suggestions for small revisions were almost always on target.

And I again want to thank my wife Cindy, who had to put up with all my time writing and researching as well as listening to my enthusiastic reports of the interesting tidbits of knowledge that I was encountering while researching and writing.

Table of Contents

More French You Use Without Knowing It

This is not a book with useful facts to memorize. In fact it's probably not useful at all. It's interesting. It's fun to read. It will stretch your mind and introduce you to things you never imagined. Think of reading these fascinating stories just as a pleasure you grant yourself when you just feel like reading something interesting.

If you have read the first book in this series, *All the French You Use Without Knowing It,* you already know that these words aren't alphabetized. First of all this isn't a dictionary. Secondly, these words don't lend themselves to being alphabetized. For example, it makes more sense to group enlarge with large, and film noir with cinema, rather than to separate them alphabetically.

Nevertheless, I've included an alphabetical list of the words in the back of the book to help you return to a word you found particularly interesting.

Now let's go ahead and get started with our first word.

very

The English word **very** came from the Old French word **verai, verrai** or **verray** way back in the middle 13th century. In fact, at the time, very started off being written verrai in English.

What is very interesting is that the Old French **verai** was an adjective meaning <u>true</u>, <u>real</u>, or <u>genuine</u>.

Eventually, the **e** in **verai** was elided and then dropped, giving the current French word **vrai**, which of course still means <u>true</u>, <u>real</u>, or <u>genuine</u> in Modern French.

Thus **very** is a close cousin of the word *vrai* in French, and a cousin of verify (to make sure something is true) and of verification (proof that something is true), and of veritable and of veracity, in English.

Very started off **in English** as an adjective meaning <u>true</u>, <u>real</u>, or <u>genuine</u> (the same meaning that *verai* had in French). Here's a quote from Shakespeare to illustrate:

Like very sanctity she did approach.

Very wasn't used to mean <u>greatly</u> or <u>extremely</u> until the 15th century, but has been used to <u>intensify</u> ever since.

In English now, **very** is often used as an **adverb** intensifiying, as in :

very happy, very big --- (extremely happy, extremely big).

Thinking back to very as once upon a time meaning

true, real or genuine, note that you could also translate very big as truly, really, or genuinely big. It's only a tiny difference in meaning, if any at all.)

> He plays very well --- (extremely well, really well).

> the very worst thing you could do --- (truly the worst, absolutely the worst, really the worst).

> It's the very same place --- (It's truly the same place, etc.).

Besides being an adverb, **very** is also still used as an **adjective** meaning true, real, precise, actual or absolute (again demonstrating its origins and its relationship to *vrai*).

> the very end of his life

> the very center of the city

> the very thing I needed

> the very opposite

> the very image of his brother

Note: The word "true" means in accordance with fact or reality. For example, consider the following very simple sentence. "That's true". The word "very" couldn't be used in place of true in this sentence to mean the same thing. Nor could it be used in the sentence "I believe his testimony to be true", nor any other similar sentence.

Thus very can't necessarily replace true. However, true or truly (or real or really) can replace very in almost all cases, with little or no alteration in meaning.

In other words, true, truly, real and really can usually be used as synonyms for **very**, which isn't too surprising considering that very's original meaning was true or real.

veracity
verify
verity
veritable
verification

These words are all related to the Old French word **verai** (meaning true, real or genuine), that gave birth to **very** and **vrai**. We'll cover them fairly rapidly.

1. Veracity is a fairly new word in English, coming from the French **véracité** in the 1600's. Both words have kept the same meaning: truth, accuracy, exactness.

The French **véracité** actually started out as a word coming from religious dogma. La véracité de Dieu expressed a dogma that God could never be wrong, that He could never make a mistake. It wasn't until the 1700's that **véracité** began being used in non-religious contexts.

2. Verify is an older word, coming from **vérifier** in the 14th or 15th century. While **véracité** started as a religious word, **vérifier** started as a legal word, meaning to endorse, ratify or approve some act or official paper (in declaring that it was correct and genuine).

Thus, **verify** also entered English as a legal word. Later on, its meaning expanded in both languages to mean to <u>check the accuracy of something</u> in a general sense. For example:

>We verified his conclusions --- *On a vérifié ses conclusions.*

However, to verify still has a legal meaning in addition to its general meaning. In the legal sense, to verify is to swear to, or to support a statement by an affidavit.

3. Verity is a rather literary word meaning truth in English. It came from the Old French **verite** (which is now **vérité** in Modern French), in the late 1300's. The French word *verite*, itself, came from an earlier Old French word, *verté* or *vertet*.

The French **vérité** *(verite)* started out as a <u>philosophic</u> word meaning Truth with a capital T. That is Truth meaning a true principle or belief, which has an internal coherence, and is presumed to be of great or fundamental importance. **Verity** and **vérité** have kept this sense in both languages:

>the eternal verities --- *les vérités éternelles*

However, in French, **la vérité** is also the standard, everyday word for truth in general. In English, on the other hand, **verity** can mean ordinary truth but it's a very formal and literary way of saying it. In English you are much more likely to say "truth" than "verity".

Side Note: The expression **cinema vérité** (with the French spelling) was borrowed in the 1960's to describe a genre of film and television programs emphasizing realism and naturalism. Below is a definition from Wikipedia:

> Cinéma vérité is a style of documentary film-making combining naturalistic techniques with stylized cinematic devices of editing and camerawork, staged set-ups, and the use of the camera to provoke subjects.

4. Veritable came into English from French twice. First in the late 1400's from **véritable**, which itself had come from *vérité*. Then it apparently almost died out in English after the mid 1600's and was re-imported or revived sometime after 1830.

At first, **veritable** and **véritable** meant <u>true</u>, <u>believable</u> or <u>speaking the truth</u>, as in:

> *un homme véritable* --- a veritable man, a man who you can believe

> *pour vous montrer que je suis véritable* --- to show you that I am believable, veritable.

> *Oh, si c'est véritable !* --- Oh, if that's only true, believable, veritable!

However now, in both languages, that sense is fairly

obsolete and veritable and *véritable* are used more as intensifiers and mean authentic, genuine, real, or true.

> *C'est une véritable catastrophe* --- It's a veritable catastrophe (real, genuine).

> *Il s'agissait d'une véritable épidémie* --- It was (or it was becoming) a veritable epidemic. (a true, real, or genuine epidemic)

5. Verification is a somewhat newer word, coming from the Old French ***vérification*** in the early 1500's. Verification pretty much has the same meaning in both languages, which is the establishment of the truth or accuracy of something, the act or process of verifying.

Verification is especially used for official documents, or making sure that the things agreed on in treaties are being carried out, and in philosophy, establishing the proof of a proposition by empirical means. In French, the *vérification* of an edict was also the recording or registering of it by *parlement*.

fuel

The English word **fuel** has an interesting history. It entered Middle English as feuel or fewel from the Old French word *feuaile, fouaille, fouail, fuwaille, feuwelle,* or *fuail* (a word which meant small pieces of firewood). The dominant spelling seems to have been ***fouaille***, and the verb ***fouailler*** meant to burn (something) in a fire.

In English, over the years, the spelling simplified from feuel and fewel to **fuel**.

Odd Historical Note: In Old French, the word *fouail* (spelled without a final *le)* also meant the parts of a *sanglier* (wild boar) which were cooked and given to the hunting dogs after the chase as their share (usually the internal organs).

In Modern French, the spelling of this hunting word has changed to *fouaille*, and the original meaning of *fouaille* as firewood has become obsolete. Firewood is now simply called *bois de chauffage*.

Another Interesting Note: To close the circle, in the 1920's *fuel-oil*, later shortened to *fuel*, came back into French from English. The French word *fuel* refers to *mazout* or home heating oil. The preferred Frenchified spelling of *fuel* is *fioul*, but both can be seen in modern French.

Thus, to retrace our steps, this word which started out as the Old French word *fouaille* (with multiple other spellings), and which meant **firewood**, entered English and became **fuel**. The word *fouaille* died out and now only retains a peculiar vestige of its previous meaning, derived from hunting. Then, less than a hundred years ago, fuel was reintroduced into French from English, as *fuel*, with the meaning of **home heating oil**, and the spelling of fuel has been turned into a French spelling, by changing it into *fioul*. What an interesting trail!

How to think about Old French spellings:

Spelling is now standardized in both French and English and we tend to think of words in terms of how they are spelled. To us, the word for the color red is r-e-d and not readde, rede, redd, read or redde.

It's important to remember, however, that at the time when many words were coming from Old French into English only a tiny proportion of the population could read, spelling wasn't standardized, and words were thought of in terms of their sounds, not their spelling. People spoke words that were sounds, not letters, just as children do now, long before they can read.

Remember, there was <u>no such thing</u> as standard spelling!

People who could write, spelled words according to how they had seen them spelled before, and barring that, they sounded them out in their heads, and spelled them according to how they had heard them, or how they would say them.

Thus the spelling of a word could vary from region to region, even from village to village, and from person to person within the village, and even from day to day for the same writer (as he probably didn't keep a record of how he had spelled the word previously).

This is why dictionaries of Old French give a list of spellings for a word (such as *feuaile, fouaille, fouail, fuwaille, feuwelle, fuail,* and others that I left out), even though they all meant the same thing. If you sound them out to yourself, you'll see that they all pretty much <u>sound</u> the same, although the spellings vary all over the lot!

It wasn't any different for English, of course. Eventually, over centuries, and especially with the influence of the printing press, spelling became more and more uniform, and one form of the word won out.

What's important to remember when you see a bunch of alternate spellings for a word, is that they are not different words. They are all the **<u>same oral word</u>**! What you are seeing are just a bunch of different, and sometimes imaginative, ways of **<u>transcribing</u>** that oral word, transcribing what the word sounds like! For people back then, the spelling for red would have been anything that sounded like "red" when you sounded it out, and was not restricted to the letters r-e-d.

fait accompli

The New Oxford American Dictionary built into my Mac defines a fait accompli like this: "a thing that has already happened or been decided before those affected hear about it, leaving them with no option but to accept".

It's usually worded that someone is "presented with" a fait accompli. For example:

They had already announced the decision and

we were thus presented with a fait accompli. (It was too late for us to do anything about it).

It's pretty clear where fait accompli comes from as it is standard everyday French. In French, **un fait** is a fact and **accompli** means accomplished, and thus **un fait accompli** is an accomplished fact.

A **fait accompli** entered English fairly recently, in the mid 1800's, but it has become an integral part of the language. It's found in literary English but you could just as well hear it in casual conversation. For example, here are a couple of snatches of conversation that you could overhear in quite informal speech:

My wife had already filed for divorce and I was hit with a fait accompli!

Sorry we don't have anything to go with the drinks. We were presented with a fait accompli when our cat ate the sardine spread off the hors d'oeuvres just before you arrived! It was too late to make anything else.

ruse

The English noun **a ruse** came into the language in the early 1400's, meaning at that time a trick that a hunted animal would use to escape from the hunters. It came from the French noun *ruse*, with the same meaning.

The French *ruse* itself was a very old word, dating from the 1200's, and part of the family of French words associated with the French verb *ruser* which meant, for a hunted animal, to dodge and use tricks to try to escape, and thus, to use trickery.

In English currently, **a ruse** has become more generalized and refers to a trick or action designed to fool someone.

> They used the ruse of telling everyone they'd be gone for the weekend so that they could have a private weekend at home without interruptions.

In current French, *une ruse* in hunting can still mean an animal's attempts to fool his pursuers. In common use *une ruse* is a trick just as in English.

> *Il a utilisé une ruse pour éviter de payer* --- He used a ruse in order to avoid paying.

Finally *la ruse* or *ruse* by itself refers to trickery or cunning.

> *Il a utilisé la ruse pour gagné* --- He used trickery (or cunning) to win.

> *Il a gagné par ruse* --- He won by trickery (or cunning).

Note that using *la ruse* this way isn't the same as saying "the trick". It doesn't refer to a single trick. It's more general and refers to the whole art of trickery or cunning. You wouldn't use ruse this way in English. In English you'd have to say "by trickery" or "by cunning".

Let's continue with the family of words in French.

The <u>verb</u> **ruser** is still used in French, although it's less common than the noun. It means to use trickery or cunning.

> *C'est une mauvaise situation. Peut-être faut-il ruser un peu* --- It's a bad situation. Maybe we need to use a little bit of trickery.

The <u>adjective</u> **rusé** (feminine **rusée**) is the most commonly seen member of the family. It means crafty, cunning, and tricky, and is used all the time in French.

> *C'est un homme rusé* --- He's a cunning (or tricky) guy.

However, the verb *ruser* and the adjective *rusé* didn't make it into English. It's only the noun *une ruse* that crossed over into our language.

film noir

The term **film noir** is interesting as it was a name given by French film critics (especially Nino Frank, Raymond Borde and Etienne Chaumeton) in the 1950's to a genre of American detective, crime, and gangster films of the 40's and 50's.

The French term *film noir* literally means "black cinema", and these were dark films, marked often by pessimism, cynicism and fatalism. They were often, but not always, filmed in black and white, and they were often literally dark, with black shadows and little light.

The term especially referred to films based on the hardboiled detective novels of the era, such as those written by Dashiell Hammett (Sam Spade, etc.), and the works of directors such as Orson Wells and Fritz Lang.

The expression **film noir** was incorporated into English where it remains today, still used to refer to films of this genre of any era. The term **film noir** has actually since spread around the world and it would be recognized by people familiar with cinematography anywhere.

cinema
cinematography
cinematic

As with words like discotheque, stereotype, and even telegraph, which I discussed in the first book in this series, *All The French You Use Without Knowing It*, I felt like I wandered into a magical treasure house when I started researching this word.

It turns out that the English word **cinema** came from the French word *cinéma* in 1899, as the word for a movie hall, or place where movies were shown.

The French word *cinéma*, in turn, was an abbreviation of the word *cinématographe*, invented by the Lumière brothers, for the apparatus that they invented in 1895 which could capture movement by a series of photographs.

The Lumière brothers were among the first to invent a movie camera and a movie projector. Their inventions were considered the true birth of moving pictures as a mass medium. They coined the word *cinématographie* the same year, and it came into English as **cinematography** (the art and science of making films), in 1897.

Historical Note: I had never heard of the Lumière brothers, but when I told my college student daughter about them she said "Oh sure, I studied about them in my film course. They're considered the fathers of cinematography". (In fact, they even originated the word, as I noted above).

Wikipedia and the Britannica Concise Encyclopedia confirmed what my daughter had said. Here's a brief summary:

The Lumière brothers, Louis and August grew up in Lyon, where their father was a painter and award winning photographer and ran a photographic business. Both boys were sent to the best technical school in Lyon and then went to work in their father's business. Louis trained in physics and August in chemistry and biology, but they worked together on their inventions.

Louis improved the dry plate process and their new dry plates were a great improvement from the limiting wet plates, and from earlier attempts at dry plates. They were also an important step towards moving pictures.

Sales of their new photographic plates boomed.

They sold a few thousand in 1882, a million a year by 1886, and 15 million a year by 1894. This gave them the financial security they needed when they took over the business in 1892 when their father retired, and they started to experiment with making moving pictures.

The Lumières patented a number of important processes. Of note is the film perforations that allow the film to advance through the camera and the projector. The **cinématographe**, a combined device which could both take pictures and project them, was patented in 1895, and their first history-making public showing (at which admission was charged) was held at *Le Grand Café* in Paris in December, 1895. Ten 50 second films were shown, with subjects as varied as workers leaving their factory at Lyon, to bathing in the sea and baby's breakfast. The first of these films, *Workers Leaving the Lumière Factory,* is considered the first true motion picture.

They followed this by making more than 40 films the next year, recording documentaries of everyday French life. They also made the first newsreels, sending out crews to record the news.

The brothers left on a world tour in 1896, with their *cinématographe* machine, visiting London, New York, Buenos Aires and Bombay among others, and created a sensation which had an immediate and powerful influence on popular culture.

They then started work on color photography and patented the Autochrome Method which was recognized as the best method for color photography until the mid 1930's.

Side Note: Edison's device, the Kinetoscope, which slightly predated the Lumières, was known as a "peep box" as just one person at a time could look into a little box and see a moving picture. The Lumières realized that it was necessary to project the images on a screen to make it a useful media. Edison disdained film projection as financially non-viable, and it really was the Lumières who were the fathers of motion pictures as a media.

Another Side Note: The French noun *cinématique* was invented in 1834 from the Greek word for movement, and *la cinématique* designated the part of the science of mechanics which studied movement. In the early 1900's, with the use of **cinema** referring to motion pictures, **cinematic** began being used as an adjective in English, meaning related to motion pictures.

niche

The French verb *nicher* dated from the 1100's and meant (and still means) to make one's nest. It's used primarily for birds.

> *Les moineaux nichent partout ici* --- The sparrows have nests everywhere around here.

The noun *niche*, which dated from the 1300's and originally meant nest, became used more and more figuratively. Eventually the word for a birds nest became *un nid*, while the figurative meanings stuck to *niche*.

In French *une niche* now can refer to a recess in a wall to display a statue, a statuette, a vase, or some other ornament. It can also just be a little alcove off a room:

> Le deuxième lit était dans une niche.

Une niche can also refer to a dog-house, or a little corner in the house where the dog has his bed.

Finally, and very figuratively, *une niche* can be a place where one fits in comfortably, as in:

> *Une niche écologique* --- an ecological niche

> *Une niche de marché* --- a market niche

The English word **niche** didn't come from French until the 17th century, when ***niche*** already had the figurative meaning of a recess in a wall. It has since taken on others:

> They put the vase in a niche especially con-structed in the wall.

> He's found his niche in the study of ancient Chinese pottery.

> It's an excellent market niche.

> That ecological niche is occupied in Australia by kangaroos.

The usual pronunciation of niche in English is with a short "i" but the French pronunciation is also heard ("neesh").

an introductory note to a family of words:

The Old French verb *alier* (also spelled *aliier, aliere, aloier, alaier, aleier, alayer, aloyer,* and *allier),* has spawned a large family of words in French, and in English as well.

The verb **alier** meant to <u>combine</u> or <u>unite</u>. It came from an earlier word **aleier** meaning to <u>combine two metals</u>, or to mix one metal with a baser metal. Eventually, over the years, with the standardization of spelling, all these alternate forms settled on **allier**, which became the dominant and standard spelling, and which even today is the current spelling of the word.

As I said, there are a number of English words coming from this verb. Let's start with the English word alloy.

an alloy
to alloy

The noun **alloy** came into English about the year 1600 from the French **aloi** (or *alei),* given as a past participle of the now obsolete verb *aloier* or *aloyer.* As noted above, the verb *aloier* and its alternate forms *aloyer, aleir, aliere, aloir* and *aleier,* have long since been folded into the Modern French **allier**.

In French, *aloi* dated from the 1200's. It was most often used for combining other metals with gold and silver, especially gold or silver coins. Saying that the coins were *de bon aloi* meant that they were of the correct percentage of precious metal (and hence of good quality). On the other hand, *de bas aloi* meant that they had been adulterated.

The noun *aloi* could even be used figuratively, as in:

> *Un homme de bas aloi* --- someone of low birth, low condition or a low profession.

> *Marchandise de mauvais aloi* --- merchandise that didn't come up to requirements or regulations.

While in current French, *aloi* is pronounced "alwa", if you were to sound out the letters the way one would in English, you can see where "alloy" comes from.

The verb **to alloy** came into English about 60 years after the noun, from the same French family of verbs.

Since all the various spelling for these related French verbs have since settled into the single form *allier*, the current French verb meaning to alloy is **allier** *(al-oier* is obsolete as noted above). Thus the current French noun for an alloy is no longer *un aloi*, but **un alliage.**

Although *aloier* is long gone, **aloi** has hung on as a vestige word in modern French. While its use to mean an alloy is now obsolete, **aloi** is still the legal word for the titer or percentage of gold or silver in coins, or in silverware, for instance. And *de bon aloi* or *de mauvais aloi* still is used locally to mean of good or of bad quality.

Historical Note: It's interesting to note that although "to make an alloy" was the original and oldest meaning for these verbs in French, and dated from the 1100's to 1200's, the word alloy didn't arrive in English until 1600. On the other hand, other derivative meanings which we will cover below, such as **to ally**, seem to have arrived in English much earlier.

Let's continue first with the verb to ally (with).

to ally

You've probably already guessed that, like to alloy, the verb **to ally** comes from the ***allier*** family of French verbs. To ally made its first appearance in English many centuries ago in the sense of to combine or unite (at first in referring to metals).

The English word **to ally** continued to be influenced by *allier* as *allier* started to be used in figurative senses in French, and thus **to ally** separated from **to alloy**.

For example *allier* had started to be used not just for metals, but for people and families who were joining each other by marriage (combining figuratively). Here are some examples from the dictionary of the *Académie française* from 1694 (Please excuse any archaic sentence structure. It's from the dictionary):

Il veut se bien allier.

Il veut s'allier à une bonne famille.

Il veut s'allier avec une bonne famille.

A bit later *s'allier* also began to be used in the political sense, referring to countries or princes allying themselves with each other.

The example just below is from the same 1694 dictionary. The spelling, grammar, and capitalization are different from what we'd see in current-day French, and not yet fully standardized, but the meaning is plain: ***allier*** had changed from just referring to metals being combined, to now referring to families, countries, princes or estates becoming allied.

> *On le dit aussi des Princes & des Estats qui entrent en ligue & traitent ensemble pour leur commune deffense:* Ces deux Republiques s'allierent ensemble. Ces deux Rois se sont al-liez. C'est l'interest de leurs Estats qui les allie.

allied

The adjective **allied** appeared in English about the same time as the verb to ally, coming from ***alie,*** the past participle of ***alier*** from Old French. (Sometimes these Old French words didn't have the accent that they would have in Modern French. I didn't forget the accent on *alie*, for instance. It's how the words were written back then.) It was originally used in the sense of families being allied by marriage, but began to be used for political treaties or leagues about century later.

an ally

The noun, an **ally**, in the sense of one who was allied with another by a treaty or commitment came along several centuries after the verb to ally. It was partly influenced by the Old French *alie* (allied), and partly by the then already existing English verb, to ally.

The current French word for allied has changed to *allié* as a result of *alier* folding into *allier*, and of spelling becoming more uniform. The current French word for an ally has changed as well to *un allié*.

> *La France et l'Angleterre étaient alliées* --- France and England were allied / were allies.

> *Les Alliés* --- The Allies (the countries allied against Germany during World War I and World War II).

> *Elle a trouvé en lui un allié* --- She has found an ally in him.

alliance

The noun **alliance** comes, of course, from the same group of words. First used in English about the year 1300, it came from the Old French *aliance* (or *aleiance),* coming from the verb *alier*. As *alier* added an L to change to *allier* in modern French, *aliance* has become *alliance*.

As you might expect from our discussion of the verb to ally above, an **alliance** was first used in English in the sense of families forming an alliance by marriage, and only later taking on the political sense.

Note: While alliance started in English as a word referring to an alliance between families by marriage, in Modern English, to use alliance to refer to a marriage would be a very literary, historical, and rather rarified way of using the word. My computer's built in New Oxford American Dictionary doesn't even mention it, nor does the Merriam Webster Online Dictionary (although older dictionaries from 1982 and 1913 do). The current usage primarily is political, military or interpersonal (for example two countries, two companies, or two businessmen forming an alliance).

In French, however, *une alliance* continues to betray its history. For example, while *une alliance* can mean a political or business alliance, it often refers to marriage:

> *Elle est sa parente par alliance* --- She's his relative by marriage.

> *Il essaie d'entrer par alliance dans une des grandes familles* --- He's trying to enter one of the great families (of France) by marriage.

And to prove the point, a wedding ring is *une alliance* in French.

color

The noun **color** came from the Old French **color** (now **couleur** in Modern French) in the early 14th century, at which time **color** primarily meant complexion or color of the skin. The current spelling of **couleur** was already adopted in French dictionaries by the early 1600's, if not before.

While we are on the subject of colors, the colors blue, orange, beige, chartreuse, rose and violet, among others, are also from French. We discussed violet earlier (in *All the French You Use Without Knowing It)*. Let's now discuss some others briefly.

blue

Blue came from the Old French **bleu** around 1300. *Bleu* was also spelled *blo, blwe* and *bloi* and had a number of separate meanings besides blue. In fact, it seems to have also meant pale or wan, or blond, as well as blue. **Bleu** eventually settled on blue for its sole meaning, and it still means blue.

orange

The English word **orange** came from the Old French word **orenge** or **pomme d'orenge** back in the 1300's somewhere. At that time it was the name of the fruit and not yet used for the color. In fact it wasn't used for the color orange (the color of the fruit) until about 1550, two hundred years later.

In both English and French the spelling is now **orange**, and ***orange*** is the name for both the color and the fruit in both languages.

Side note: An orange tree is called *un orangier* in French.

Historical Note: The French word *orange* came from the Italian *arancia*, which was originally *narancia*, or *naranza* in Venitian.

beige
serge

Beige is a pale, sandy yellowish-brown color. It didn't enter English until modern times, about 1860, coming from the French adjective ***beige*** which dated from the 1200's.

The French word ***beige*** itself started off as a <u>noun</u> referring to a serge (twilled) fabric made from wool. In the 1798 edition of the *Dictionnaire de l'Académie française,* the word beige was still defined only in this way, as a serge fabric made of wool.

By the 1835 edition, French had started to use ***beige*** either as an <u>adjective</u> which referred to wool that still had its natural color *(laine beige),* or as a <u>noun</u> where *beige* still meant serge fabric, but a serge fabric made from undyed wool which still had its natural color. Beige didn't quite mean a color yet but it was on its way.

In Modern French ***beige*** is either the color used as

an adjective *(une chemise beige)* or the color itself used as a noun *(un joli beige)*. It's no longer listed as a fabric at all in my *Petit Robert.*

Historical Note: When the word "beige" was first used in English it was used as a noun referring to a <u>fabric</u>. In other words, beige meant a fabric made of unbleached and undyed wool. Its use as a <u>color</u> in English didn't start until 1880, about twenty years after its introduction into English.

The use of "beige" to mean a fabric is now a rare usage in English, as it is in French, although this sense is still listed in some English dictionaries. (Its inclusion in some dictionaries reflects the debate I commented on in my earlier book, about whether obsolete words should be dropped out of dictionaries or kept pretty much indefinitely).

Odd and Interesting Note: As you would expect, since beige entered English in the 1860's, it wasn't listed at all in the 1828 Webster's dictionary. What is interesting, however, is that the listing for the word beige in the 1913 Webster's was as a noun meaning "debeige".

I had never heard of debeige but I found it defined in a couple of current dictionaries as "de'beige': a kind of woolen or mixed dress goods". Debeige is now a totally obsolete word, but it shows that in the 1913 Webster's at least, the word **beige** was used for a fabric made "de beige". In other words, "of undyed wool". It was copied directly from the French.

When this 1913 dictionary was being prepared,

beige as a color, either as a noun (a dark beige) or as an adjective (a beige shirt), was not yet seen often enough to be accepted into the dictionary as a new word.

By the way, since beige was originally a serge fabric, we should mention that **serge** is also of French origin, coming into English in the 14th century from the French word *serge*, referring to woolen cloth mixed with silk or linen.

In English, **serge** now refers to a strong twilled fabric with a diagonal rib, made of wool, silk or possibly other fabrics, and used for suits or coats. It has the same meaning in French.

ecru

While we are on beige, the color **ecru**, which is a light beige, comes from the French *écru*. The word ecru arrived in English about the year 1870, roughly ten years after beige. The color ecru is the color of unbleached linen and is slightly lighter than beige which is the color of unbleached wool.

The word *écru* came from the Old French word *escru* meaning completely raw. *Cru,* of course, means raw in Modern French. The spelling followed the familiar path of dropping the *"s"* and adding an accent.

The original sense of *écru* referred to something which was in its natural state. However, in Modern French *écru* refers either to a fabric which is neither dyed nor bleached and has thus kept its natural color, or to the color itself.

maroon

For one last color, **maroon** (which is a reddish brown) was first used in English in the 1590's as a noun to refer to a <u>chestnut</u> from Southern France, direct from the French word ***marron***.

The idea of maroon as a very dark reddish brown <u>color</u> (chestnut color) came about two hundred years later from the French color ***marron.***

Maroon as a chestnut is now obsolete in English and isn't even listed in my dictionaries back to 1913 (although the French *marron* variety of chestnut is listed as the source of the word).

petite

The feminine French adjective ***petite*** (little or small) has been used in English since the late 1700's to describe a woman who is small and (usually) slender. It's usually a complimentary term.

She was a petite, energetic woman.

It's been used as a clothing size for women since 1929, again referring to short (and usually thin) sizes.

Is this dress available in petite?

petty

While we are on the subject, **petty** is an English phonetic spelling of the French *petit*, meaning <u>small</u>. It was first used in English in about 1400, probably at the time simply as a result of misspelling.

Petty was generalized to mean <u>of small importance</u> in the 1500's.

> Let's not worry about petty details.

The use of petty to mean <u>small minded</u> dates from the 1580's.

> He's acting in a very petty way. (He's picking on trivial things in a mean and spiteful way).

Petty larceny refers to <u>theft</u> with a value of a <u>smaller amount</u> of money than grand larceny. It dates from the late 1600's.

Petty cash is small amounts of money kept accessible to spend on small items.

> We'll take it out of petty cash.

petit

The term **petit larceny** was used a century before petty larceny in English, and both are still used.

Petit entered English long before petty, of course, but has been replaced by petty in all but some established expressions such as **petit mal seizures** (a form of epilepsy), **petit four** (a very small pastry or cookie (literally "small oven" in French), **petit point** (a small needlepoint stitch), and **petit bourgeois** (pertaining to, or a member of, the lower middle class with an emphasis on conventionality and con-servatism). As in:

> They maintained a certain petit bourgeois re-spectability.

The **petite bourgeoisie** refers to the entire lower middle class of small shopkeepers, clerks, etc. (This is petite rather than petit but I included it here rather than under petite as it fits in here, being just the fem-inine of petit).

Interesting Side Note: You may be wondering why petit four, petit mal, petit point and petit bourgeois didn't change into petty four, petty mal, etc.

The reason is simple. Petit was anglicized into petty way back in the 1400's. From then on, petty then was an independent word with its own existence.

On the other hand, petit four, petit mal, petit point and petit bourgeois entered English recently, all in the mid 1800's, as new words. This was 400 years after petty became a free-standing word, and there was no reason to make a connection between these new words and petty.

larceny

Since we've just been talking about petit larceny, we

could guess that **larceny** also comes from French, and of course it does, from the 13th century Old French word *larcin* meaning theft. *(Larcin* came from an even older French word *larrecin*, with the same meaning).

In current French, **larcin** is a literary word referring to a small theft committed without violence, and perhaps furtively (shoplifting, for example). Synonyms for *commettre un larcin* would be *chaparder* and *dérober.*

In the past, **larcin** also could mean the object stolen (the "loot"), but that sense is now *vieilli* (obsolete).

grand

While **petit**, the French word for small, is used only in limited expressions in English (as we've indicated above), **grand**, the French word for big, is used throughout English, and in many expressions, although its sense has changed over the centuries to usually mean impressive or even awe-inspiring. When you are talking about size, the words "big" and "large" are preferred over "grand" in English.

As I suggested above, rather than just meaning big, the word **grand** in English means <u>impressive, imposing and magnificent</u>. For example, consider the following:

the Grand Hotel, the Grand Canyon,

It was on a grand scale.

Grand can also mean <u>of a higher rank or more im-</u><u>portant</u> (a grand duke, a grand piano, grand larce-ny), while in casual speech it can mean <u>excellent</u> <u>and splendid</u> (What a grand day!, That's grand!)

In French, on the other hand, *grand* remains the word for concretely <u>big or large</u> in size, whether you are talking about a foot *(un grand pied),* a fish *(un grand poisson),* or a city *(une grande ville).*

The adjective *grand* can also be used for non-concrete things. For example, consider *grand ou-vert* (wide open), *grande profondeur* (great depth), *grands événements* (great events), *grand chagrin* (great sorrow), *grand vent* (big wind), *grand intelli-gence* (wide and comprehensive knowledge).

Note that you use big, large, or great for all these ex-amples when you translate them into English, rather than grand.

In French, the word *grand* can also have a mean-ing similar to the English word great in the sense of important. You can think of *un grand vin, une grande école, un grand maître, un grand champion, un grand film de l'époque.* You would translate each of these into English by great instead of grand (a great wine, a great champion, etc).

grandeur

From which we come to the French word *grandeur*, which came from *grand* way back in the 12th cen-tury. It migrated into English as the word **grandeur** around the year 1500, in the sense of size, height, loftiness. This came from the use of *grandeur* in French in ways similar to this:

> *Il était effrayé par la grandeur du problème* --- He was frightened by the size, enormity, of the problem.

> *Il cherche des pierres d'une certaine grandeur* --- He's looking for stones of a certain size.

> *Ces deux hommes sont de la même grandeur* --- These two men are of the same height.

Note: *Grandeur* in these sentences means size. In current English **grandeur** isn't used like this. Thus all these sentences are translated into English by size or height.

In Modern French, while *grandeur* could conceivably be used in these sentences, people would be more likely use *ampleur* instead in the first sentence, and in the second sentence they would most likely use *taille* or possibly *dimensions,* and in the third sentence they might also use *taille* or *hauteur.*

Very off the topic Side Note: In the third example above we used the words *la même grandeur.* At the time we were talking about (1500), *la même grandeur* would have been written *la mesme grandeur.* As Old French changed to Modern French, an **accent**, often a circumflex, over the preceding vowel often replaced an **s** before a consonant. (For example, *mesme* became *même*, *forest* became *fôret*, and *chasteau* became *château*. There are many more.)

The enlarged meaning of greatness, grandness, majesty, stateliness, splendor and impressiveness for the French word *grandeur* wasn't used in English until the 1660's or so. In French, it's used mostly for people or things they've created, and for nobility of spirit. For example:

> *Il a un air de grandeur* --- He has an air of grandeur.

> *La grandeur de Rome* --- The grandeur of Rome.

On the other hand, the grandeur of the mountains might more likely be rendered in French as *la splendeur, la magnificence* or *la majesté*.

splendor
magnificence
magnificent
majesty

As you could tell from the last sentence of the previous section, **splendor**, **magnificence** and **majesty** are of course three French words which were hardly modified. All three entered English hundreds of years ago.

Splendor (or **splendour** in British English) was first introduced in the mid 1400's, coming from the Middle French, *esplendour, esplendeur* or *splendur*. By the end of the 1500's the French spelling had adopted its Modern French form of *splendeur*.

Magnificence came into English at about the same

time, from the Old French **magnificence** (which is still *magnificence* in Modern French). The Old French **magnificent** wasn't modified on its entrance into English either.

Majesty came around 1300 from the Old French **majeste**. It was first used in English to refer to the qualities of God, and was expanded to describe royalty a century later. The current French word is **majesté**. The English adjective **majestic** evolved from the noun majesty. (The French equivalent is *majestueux)*

gross

Gross is an interesting word and it has had an interesting journey.

The English **adjective** gross came from the Old French word for large, which was **gros** (or **grosse** in the feminine). It was first used in English in the middle 1300's, and started out meaning large, big, thick, bulky or coarse.

Over the next few hundred years, however, gross split into a number of related meanings. First of all, it maintained the sense of bulky or coarse, as in

He has rather gross features.

or unattractively large or bloated, as in

Look at that gross stomach.

However it added several additional and different

meanings in English. For its first new meaning, gross came to mean <u>flagrant, obvious, glaring</u>, as in:

He made a gross error in judgment.

That was a gross exaggeration.

You can see how this sense is a figurative use for large, big or massive, but that it has now become an intensifier for negative attributes such as "gross stupidity" or a "gross miscalculation", as well as those used in the examples above. Gross is never used in this sense to intensify a positive attribute.

In this sense gross can also be used as the **adverb** grossly as in:

He grossly exaggerated the circumstances.

The second new meaning for gross (starting in the 1500's), became <u>total or entire</u>. For example:

the gross profit (as opposed to net profit)

the gross weight (as opposed to net weight)

The Gross National Product

in gross (in total)

While up to here we've primarily discussed gross as an **adjective**, gross in its financial sense is also used as a **verb** in casual English (believe it or not). For example:

He hopes to gross $20,000 from this deal.

He grossed $200,000 last year.

This refers to profit or earnings before taxes.

Gross also developed uses as a **noun** in English. In its financial sense it means <u>earnings or profit before deductions</u>:

> My gross was... (what I earned before taxes and expenses was...).

This probably originated as an informal abbreviation of "my gross earnings" or "my gross profit".

And returning to gross as an adjective, while in "gross error" or "gross stupidity", gross is intensifying a negative attribute, in another new sense, gross expanded its original sense of <u>coarse</u> in a figurative way to mean <u>vulgar or in bad taste</u>. For example,

> gross language

> gross behavior

Note that here gross is not intensifying a negative. There is no negative, no "stupidity", "error", or "miscalculation", in these phrases. There are just neutral words like behavior and language. In this usage, it's gross itself that provides the negative.

Since the late 1950's, in adolescent slang, gross has gone further and means <u>disgusting</u>, or as a verb meaning <u>to disgust</u>, as in:

> That's gross!

That grossed me out!

And the Old French expression **une grosse dou-zaine,** meaning a "large dozen" (and thus, a dozen dozen), became **a gross** in English, also meaning a dozen dozen.

If you look back through this section you'll see that this is an incredibly rich set of meanings that has developed from a word which originally simply meant large!

The French adjective *gros* still means large, or when referring to a person, corpulent. It can also be used figuratively so that, while still meaning large, it can also mean major or important, as in

C'était une grosse chute de neige.

Il a une grosse fortune.

Une grosse fièvre

The French adjective *gros* can also mean coarse:

Il a de gros traits --- He has gross / coarse features.

or it can mean vulgar:

C'est un gros mot --- It's a vulgar word.

Gros can also be used as an **adverb**, keeping the sense of "large", in a way:

Ça coûte gros, il gagne gros, il joue gros (a lot of money).

Il vend en détail et en gros --- He sells retail and wholesale.

Finally, ***gros*** can be used as a **noun**:

Le gros de l'armée --- The majority of the army / The largest part of the army.

Qu'est-ce que nous pouvons faire contre un gros ? --- What can we do against such an influential person?

Mon gros --- (term of affection, as is *mon grand* and *mon petit)*

large

Now let's talk about the word **large**. It's another interesting word in that, while the French word *gros* means large, and the French *grand* also can mean large, the French word ***large*** does not mean large but means wide or broad. So how did the two words get where they are?

Well let's look. The French adjective ***large*** emerged a thousand years ago, in the 11th century, meaning plentiful, copious, abundant, and bountiful. **Large** migrated from French to English in the late 12th century, with that same meaning at first.

The modern meaning of large in English as physically big (a large mountain, large dog, or large spoon), or physically extensive (a large field, large lake or large city) began to be seen a hundred years later, roughly in about 1300.

Large has also kept its original meaning of <u>plentiful, abundant or copious</u> as well (a large supply, a large fortune, a large amount, a large population). "He's a large manufacturer of copper tubing" would probably fit in here as well, as it doesn't mean he's big in stature, it means he makes a lot of copper tubing, a copious supply of copper tubing.

Large has also taken other meanings in the past, meanings you might find in Chaucer, Milton or Shakespeare, which are now <u>obsolete</u>. For example:

large meaning extravagant in spending (probably related to the sense of abundant and copious)

large meaning free, unrestrained, unburdened ("He set the prisoners large") This is now obsolete and has now been somewhat replaced by the expression "at large". ("They remain at large").

large meaning unrestrained by decorum and thus vulgar, as in "large jests" (Shakespeare). Maybe an extension of the sense of unrestrained, just above.

large meaning profuse of speech "He's very large on the subject". Clearly an extension of the sense of abundant and copious. The closest we have in Modern English is "He's going to enlarge on the subject".

In French, the word *large* usually means <u>wide</u> or broad. The sense big is taken by the French words **grand** and **gros**.

> *Il a les épaules larges / Il est large d'épaules* --- He has broad shoulders.

> *C'est plus haut que large* --- It's taller than it's wide.

> *Cette route est plus large que l'autre* --- wider.

It can also be used <u>figuratively</u>:

> *J'ai utilisé ce terme dans son sens large* --- I used that term in its broad sense.

As with **large** in English, *large* in French has kept its original sense of <u>copious</u> and <u>abundant</u>. For example:

> dans une large mesure

> de larges ressources

One of the senses for large which is obsolete in English, that of spending freely, is still used in French in an idiomatic expression:

> *Il mène une vie large* --- He spends without worrying about it, he lives well, etc.

Large was used for generous or liberal (with money, gifts, etc) but the *Académie française* dictionary of 1762 said it was fairly obsolete even the*n: "Large s'est dit autrefois pour Libéral; mais en ce sens il n'a plus guère d'usage."*

And *large* can also be a <u>noun</u> in French. The noun *le large* is the <u>open sea</u>.

> *au large de* --- off the shore of

> *en regardant vers le large* --- while looking out to sea

> *prendre le large* --- take to the sea (From that it can figuratively mean run off, or escape).

Finally the noun *large* can mean <u>width</u>.

> *dix mètres de large* --- ten meters in width

largesse or largess

From large we proceed to **largesse**, which has kept the meaning of bountiful and generous. It means either a generous gift, or generosity in giving gifts, as from a patron to his subjects, or from a well-to-do person to people less wealthy. It can sometimes have the implication of ostentation but this isn't at all a necessary part of the meaning. **Largesse** is mostly a literary or historical word.

The English **largesse** came from the Old French *largesse* many hundreds of years ago, and *largesse* itself came from *large*. The noun **largesse** has the same two meanings in both languages.

> *Il profite de la largesse du roi* --- He benefits from the king's largesse. (generosity)

> *Il donne des largesses aux petits gens du vil-*

lage --- He distributes largesse to the local village people. (generous gifts)

Note: Largesse can also be spelled largess in English.

enlarge

The related English verb **to enlarge,** came in the 1400's from the Old French ***enlarger*** *(enlargier, enlargir, eslargir, élargir)* which meant to make bigger, augment, enlarge.

However, reminiscent of one of the obsolete uses of the adjective large in English which we just discussed above, from the 1300's on in legal French these same verbs *(enlarger, enlargier, enlargir, eslargir, élargir)* could also mean to set someone free from prison, to set them at liberty.

Side Note: To set someone free from prison is also listed as a meaning for enlarge in the online Merriam Webster Dictionary. I thought this was strange as I've never heard **enlarge** used this way, not ever!

To set someone free was an obsolete meaning for **enlarge** back in my 1982 Webster's. In fact it was listed as an archaic meaning even in the 1913 Webster's, but was listed as an active meaning in 1828.

There are two things of interest here. The first is that enlarge, in the sense of setting free from prison, existed in the past in both languages, even if it's obsolete now in English and only used in legalese in current French.

Secondly, whether an obsolete, no longer used word is still included in a dictionary or not reflects the ongoing, and never to be resolved, battle between traditionalists and modernists in the dictionary world.

Another Side Note: In current French, all the various spellings of the French verb meaning to enlarge have become standardized at *élargir*.

Detroit
Cadillac

There are a lot of American place names that are French words. Detroit is a prominent one.

Un détroit is the French word meaning a <u>strait</u>, which is a narrow passage of water between two large bodies of water.

In the case of the city of **Detroit**, the *détroit* was the French word for the waterway that drains the waters of Lake Huron into Lake Erie.

Hence, from the 1600's when French explorers discovered it, the entire region was referred to as *le Détroit du lac Érié.*

In 1701, *Antoine Laumet de La Mothe, sieur de Cadillac*, founded a settlement called *Fort Ponchartrain du Détroit* on the spot where Detroit is now, naming it after the then Minister of Marine under *Louis XIV*. During the French and Indian War (1760), British troops gained control of the settlement and shortened the name to **Detroit**.

The Cadillac car, the town of Cadillac in Michigan, and Cadillac Mountain in Maine, are all named after *le sieur de **Cadillac***. (In French, by the way, it's pronounced approximately "cadiyak", and not the way we pronounce it in English).

Des Moines

The city of Des Moines is another with a French name. It was apparently shortened from ***Fort des moines,*** the original settlement, which itself was named after ***Rivière des moines*** (river of the monks), now the Des Moines River.

There are theories that the French deformed the name from an American Indian word meaning river of mounds, referring to burial mounds. However the popular explanation, which indeed seems equally reasonable, is that it was named after a Trappist monk settlement which existed at the mouth of the river.

Whichever story you wish to choose, the French named the river *Rivière des moines,* and the city of Des Moines is named after the river.

courteous

The English word **courteous** arrived in the language about 1300 with the spelling **curteis**, coming directly from the Old French ***corteis, courteis,*** or ***curteis*** which meant having courtly bearing and manners.

By 1350, curteis had taken its present form in English as **courteous**, but it was a fairly rare word until about 1500. The spelling also changed In Modern French and now is *courtois* (or *courtoise* in the feminine)

court
courtyard

The Old French adjectives discussed just above, *corteis, courteis,* and *curteis,* themselves came from the Old French noun **cort, curt,** or **court** referring to a royal court or residence. (The words *cort* and *curt* are the oldest, dating from perhaps the year 1000. Then *court* emerged in the 1200's).

In Modern French the word for court is none of these three, but instead *cour,* which dates from about 1350.

The English word **court** came from the French *cort* in the 1100's and there has been a lot of parallel development of the words since.

Historical Notes: The French *cort* itself came from a Latin word meaning garden, yard, or plot of ground. This may help explain the English word **courtyard**, which is an open quadrangular space enclosed by a building or a group of buildings. This is also another meaning for the French word *cour).*

In both English and in French, **the court** and *la cour*

not only mean a <u>royal residence</u>, but the people around the king, his <u>entourage</u>.

In both languages as well, **the court** and *la cour* can mean a <u>legal tribunal</u> (perhaps because the king, at court, was the first dispenser of justice).

Another Interesting Historical Note: Consider the English word court, which had come from the French *cort* and *court*, which French words then became obsolete and changed to *cour*. This English word court (with a "t") migrated back to French in the 1860's as an Anglicism, as *un court de tennis* (the *"t"* isn't pronounced), which is a tennis court.

to court

You may wonder how we get from the noun **a court** to the verb **to court**, which at first glance seems so different.

In English, **to court** means to pay special attention to someone in order to win their favor.

> He courted the political leaders to try to get special favors.

As a special case of the above, **to court** refers to a man paying special attentions to a woman, possibly with the goal of interesting her in marriage.

> He courted her for three years before they got married.

This latter usage may be becoming a bit dated in the modern world, but it's still used in biology where **a courting ritual** can refer to a male bird or animal courting a female.

Courting danger and similar expressions, referring to seeking danger for the thrill of it, use court figuratively.

So how did we get to wooing from a kings court? Well, as we discussed above, part of the meaning of *cort*, *court* or *cour* in French (and in English) was the people who surrounded the king or another powerful person (his court), who were there in hope of getting special favors or privileges.

Thus *il fait sa cour à quelqu'un* came to mean that he's paying homage to someone as one does at court, he's trying to please the person in order to obtain favors.

This led to **Il fait la cour à Marie** meaning that he's being attentive to Marie and trying to please her (basically that he's "courting" her). In addition to the expression *faire la cour à*, there is a self sufficient verb with the same meaning, *courtiser*.

The English verb **to court** came from the French *il fait sa cour* in the mid 1500's.

courtesy
courtly
courtship
courtesan
courtier

There is a whole family of these related words, which I'll touch on briefly, before we move on to other subjects.

First, **courtesy**, from the French *curteisie* or *corteisie* (coming from *curteis* or *corteis* meaning courteous, which we discussed above).

Second, **courtly**, meaning having refined and polished manners, (as befitting someone at the royal court).

Third, **courtship**, originally meant the behavior of a person at court but started to be used for the courting of a woman in the late 1500's.

Fourth, **courtesan**, from the French *courtisane* (from the 1500's). Literally, a woman of the court, it came to mean a "kept-woman" at an elevated social status. It's now an obsolete or historical word.

Fifth, a **courtier** in English was someone who was present at court, a part of the kings court. It's probably from Old French verbs *cortoyer* or *cortoier*, to be present at court. The French word for a man of the court is different. It's not *un courtier* but *un courtisan*.

Both courtier and courtesan in English, and *courti-*

san and *courtisane* in French are historical words, currently outdated, as king's courts are no longer in fashion.

Side Note 1: *Un courtier* in French isn't a courtier but a broker. *Courtier* comes from a different direction than all the rest of our court-related words. It comes from the verb *courir*, many centuries ago. Perhaps a broker had to "run" back and forth between the people while brokering a deal. Don't confuse a courtier with *un courtier*.

Side Note 2: Also don't confuse the English word courtesan (a woman) with the French word *courtisan* (a man).

curtsy

I couldn't resist giving curtsy a section of its own. The word **curtsy** was a variant spelling of **courtesy** dating from the middle 1500's (from Old French **corteisie**), and referred to showing respect by a gesture, such as bending the knee and bowing slightly (originally for either sex). Curtsy was used in expressions like **do curtsy** (courtesy) or **make curtsy** (courtesy) and took its present meaning by the end of the century (the 16th).

Summing Up Note: The take-away from this section is that all this group of words (courteous, court, courtyard, to court, courtship, courtly, courtesy, courtesan, courtier, curtsy), with at first glance a wide variety of meanings (polite, a place enclosed by buildings, elegant and refined, wooing, a kept-woman, a man of the court, a little bow), all came from the same French stem with the meaning of having to do with a (king's) court.

mutton

If you happen to know that the French word for sheep is *mouton*, it doesn't take much imagination to figure out where the word **mutton** comes from. (It actually came into Middle English as moton from the Old French *moton*. In English the spelling later evolved to mutton and In French to the current *mouton*).

impasse

This is an easy example. The English word **impasse**, as in:

The negotiations are at an impasse --- (further progress is blocked, at a dead end)

came in the mid 1800's from the common French word *impasse*. In French an *impasse* is a dead-end street. You'll often see streets named *"Impasse quelque chose"* just as you'd see *"Rue quelque chose"*.

pistol

The English word pistol came in the mid 1500's from the now-obsolete French word *pistole*. The current French word for a pistol is *un pistolet*. (Totally off the subject: *un pistolet* can also be a kind of bread whose form can vary according to region).

Let me tell you a few words about une pistole:

First an **arquebus** (sometimes spelled harquebus) was an early precursor of a musket, and finally of a rifle. Some were larger, mounted on a tripod, and the tripod mounted on a wagon (like a very small cannon). The rifle-size arquebuses were muzzle-loaded, could pierce armor at close range, and thus eventually led to the end of personal armor.

Well, ***une pistole*** was a small arquebus, adapted to be used with one hand, so that a soldier on horseback could use it, probably the size of a sawed-off shotgun. ***Un pistolet*** was even smaller, probably the size of a pistol.

This quote, shortened from a French dictionary of 1606, *Le Thresor de la langue francoyse* by Jean Nicot, will explain it better than I ever could:

Pistole, Est une espece de harquebouse à rouët, courte et maniable à une seule main pour en tirer. Instrument de guerre pour gens de cheval depuis qu'ils ont quitté la lance. Elle est plus grande que le pistolet.

(A *rouët* is a little wheel, which when rubbed against a flint, produced sparks to fire the weapon).

By the time of the publication of the first edition of the

Dictionnaire de l'Académie française in 1694 (the end of the same century), *une pistole* was already obsolete as a firearm, and the only *pistole* listed was a Spanish gold coin.

As for a **pistolet**, here's a quote from the same 1606 French dictionary that says it all:

> *Pistolet, Est une espece de harquebouse plus courte, plus legere et plus maniable à une main que la Pistole, et est commun à gens de pied et de cheval.*

Une pistolet has remained a pistol ever since.

Historical Side Note: Arquebuses were used by the Ming armies in China in the 1300's. The first extensive military use in Europe was in the Hungarian "Black Army" in the late 1400's. They had one of every three soldiers with an arquebus in among their pikemen, and the arquebuses were apparently effective against cavalry and even other infantry. Arquebuses soon spread throughout Europe.

fusilier
fusil
fusillade

The very old French word **fusil** referred to a piece of steel with which one hit a piece of flint to make sparks to start a fire. By 1630 *le fusil* was the support plate or tinderbox for the flint in a firearm.

Arquebuses were used in warfare in Europe during the late 1400's, the 1500's and 1600's. By about

1630 a light flintlock arquebus or musket began to be called **un mousquet à fusil**. This was then shortened to just **fusil** and a soldier armed with *un fusil* was a **fusilier**. The French Royal *Fusiliers* were organized in 1671 under Louis XIV and became a model for Europe. **Fusilier** entered English about 1680. **Fusil** had crossed the English channel some time before.

A **fusil** is now only a historical word in English, but **Fusilier** has continued to be used for members of several British regiments formerly armed with fusils. For example, a member of the Royal Scots Fusiliers, the Northumberland Fusiliers or the Royal Welch Fusiliers. Note that in English the pronunciation of Fusilier is changed and is roughly: "few-zil-leer".

The French verb **fusiller** used to mean to shoot a *fusil*. This is now a rare usage, but the verb **fusiller** is still used in French for executing a condemned person by a firing squad.

The noun **fusillade** however originated in 1770 to designate a volley of fire from *fusils*. It entered English in 1801 with the same spelling, as the word **fusillade**, meaning a volley of firearms, and is still used.

Here are a few helpful descriptions taken from a French dictionary of 1787, *Dictionaire critique de la langue française,* an excellent work by Jean-François Féraud:

*Fusilier, soldat qui a pour arme un fusil. Il ne se dit que de l'infanterie. "Compagnie de **fusiliers**".*

*Fusiller, tuer à coups de fusil un soldat condamné à être pâssé par les armes. "On a **fusillé** trois déserteurs".*

In Modern French, a **fusil** is a rifle.

a rifle
to rifle

The Old French verb **rifler** meaning to scratch or make grooves in, was used in French by 1635 in the sense of rifling, or cutting spiral grooves in a gun barrel, to make the projectile spin and thus fly more accurately to the target.

In English it became an adjective in talking about a "rifled" gun, meaning one with spiral grooves in a long barrel. This was shortened to just a **rifle**. By about 1770, a **rifle** was used in English for a shoulder weapon with a long rifled bore, while the French kept the word **fusil**.

The Old French verb **rifler** had another meaning: to steal and plunder, and **to rifle** entered English in that sense in the 1300s. In current English it means to hurriedly search through in order to find something to steal. For example:

He rifled through the drawers looking for money or jewelry.

Curious Note: The by now English noun, **rifle** (the firearm), returned to French in the 1830's as *un rifle* referring to an English carbine.

carbine
carabinier or carabineer

And to turn around again in the other direction, the English word **carbine** came in the early 1600's from the French *une carabine*, a light musket with a short barrel, carried by cavalry.

Un carabinier is a historical French word for a soldier armed with a carabine, usually on horseback. Basically a mounted musketeer.

A **carabinier** (or **carabineer**) entered English from the French as a word for a cavalry soldier armed with a carabine. It's now also an historical word in English. These soldiers were also called dragoons in English.

Side Note: Some elite <u>infantry</u> regiments were also called carabiniers in many European armies in the 1800's and even afterwards.

Another Side Note:

In **Italy**, the *carabinieri* (each individual is called a *carabiniere),* is the National Police Force (the equivalent of the *gendarmes* in France.

In **Spain**, *carabineros* became frontier guards (customs officers), currently disbanded.

Columbia, Chile, Belgium, Monaco and other countries have had, or still have, units of carabiniers.

dragoon

I mentioned just above that a dragoon was an alternate word in English for a carabinier or carabineer.

Incredibly, the English word **dragoon** for a carabinier came from a fanciful French word for *un carabinier*, **un dragon,** because their *carabines* supposedly breathed fire like a dragon. (It may have been the gun itself that was originally called *le dragon*, for the same reason, that is: breathing fire).

I'm not making it up. It's true! My Petit Robert gives **un dragon** as a historical word for *un soldat de cavalerie,* and gives as an example:

> *expéditions des dragons contre les hugenots, sous Louis XIV*

And my English dictionaries give **dragoon** as coming from the French ***dragon*** in the early 1600's.

fuselage

I wondered whether fuselage might be related in some odd way to the group of "fusil" words although it's spelled with an "e" instead of an "i". Fuselage just looked French.

Well **fuselage**, which means the body of an airplane,

did come from French, but much more recently, and from another direction. It was first documented in English about 1910, coming from **fuselage**, which was first documented in French a year or two earlier.

Fuselage in turn came from the French verb **fuseler**, which meant to shape something into the form of a **fuseau** or spindle. *Un fuseau* is the modern word for *un fusel* which was Old French and is now obsolete.

I just mentioned that the Old French word for a spindle was **un fusel**. The adjective **fuselé,** which means spindle-shaped, came from *fusel* in the 14th century, and *fuselé*, apparently, is where the verb **fuseler** originally came from.

Historical Note: In a French dictionary of the 1870's, **fuseler** was listed as an architectural word, meaning to shape anything from a column to a candelabra in a spindle shape. The verb dated from the 1840's.

A Very Side Note: When my daughter was eleven or twelve, she became interested in lace-making while we were in France. She took some lessons and joined a group of women lace-makers (hobbyists) in which she was the only non-adult. They made lace *(dentelle)* using up to forty bobbins or more at a time, which were spindle-shaped and called **fuseaux.** What they were making was called *dentelle aux fuseaux*.

Final Note: Fuselage is another "orphan" word, which is a member of a considerable family of words in French, but which is the only member of the family to be adopted into English.

potpourri

Un pot-pourri was a French word dating from the mid 1500's and referring to a *ragoût* or stew *made* from mixed (and presumably left-over) meats and vegetables. I say presumably left-over as *pot-pourri* literally means rotten-pot.

The word **potpourri** was first used in English in the beginning of the 1600's with the same meaning, a stew made from mixed meats and vegetables.

The idea of a *pot-pourri* as a collection of mixed things led to other expanded uses, specifically as a collection of dried flowers and spices first recorded in French in the early 1600's and in English in about 1750.

The use of *pot-pourri* for a medley of musical pieces was first recorded in French in 1605, and first recorded in English in 1855.

The use of *pot-pourri* for a stew is now obsolete in both languages.

blasé

The English word **blasé** came of course from the French *blasé*. It was first used in English in about 1820.

In English, to be **blasé** about something means to be bored and unable to feel emotion or pleasure because of having seen or experienced the same thing so many times before.

In French, **blasé** is the past participle of the verb **blaser**, to satiate or cloy by overindulgence.

The verb **blaser** is a literary word dating from the 1700's. The verb wouldn't be much used (if at all) in current conversation. Even in a literary sense *blaser* is probably mostly used as the past participle, *blasé*.

> Il était blasé par sa vie luxueuse.

Historical Note: When the verb blaser started out in the 1700's it referred to someone wearing themselves out by the abuse of alcohol. Later, in a figurative sense, *blasé* began to refer to other pleasures and sensations and the reference to alcohol abuse became dated and is no longer even mentioned.

Here's an excerpt from the dictionary of *l'Académie française* back in 1762:

> Blaser, se blaser: S'user à force de boire des liqueurs fortes. *Il a tant bu d'eau-de-vie qu'il s'est blasé.* Blaser est aussi actif. *Les excès l'ont blasé.*
>
> Il s'emploie figurément. *Il est blasé sur les plaisirs, sur les spectacles.*

On the other hand, in my current *Petit Robert*, alcohol abuse isn't even mentioned, except as far as etymology, and the definition is given as:

Atténuer (une sensation, une émotion) par l'abus.

In my *Harraps Shorter Dictionnaire* the definition is given as:

blaser: to make blasé

se blaser, to become blasé, to become indifferent to.

No mention of alcohol abuse here either.

avenue

The word **avenue** came from the French *avenue* in about 1600. It has had an interesting history. *Avenue* was the feminine past participle of the now extinct Old French verb *avenir* which meant to <u>come</u>, or to <u>arrive</u> *(à-venir).*

At first *l'avenue* meant the <u>act of approaching</u>, the <u>way or place of access</u> or the <u>way of approach</u>, and it started as a military word.

The meaning gradually shifted to mean the <u>driveway</u>, lined with trees, <u>leading up to</u> a country house (now called an *allée* in French). Then, by the end of the 1650's, it could refer to a broad tree-lined roadway, and by 1860, to a wide main street in a big city, especially in American English and in French.

Here's an interesting excerpt of the definition of *avenuë* from the first dictionary of *l'Académie française* in 1694. You can see the earlier uses, both military and civilian, illustrated:

> *Passage, endroit par où on arrive en quelque lieu :* *Les gardes estoient rangées à toutes les avenuës du Palais. l'armée se saisit de toutes les avenuës des montagnes. fermer, boucher les avenuës. les avenuës de cette ville sont belles.*

> *aussi* *Une allée plantée d'arbres au devant d'une maison :* *Il y a une grande avenuë qui conduit à sa maison. il a planté une avenuë d'ormes devant la porte de son chasteau.*

Side Note 1: The verb *avenir* no longer exists and in Modern French **avenir** is just a noun meaning the future. It's a common and widely used word:

> *dans l'avenir* --- this literally means in the time "to come" (the future).

Side Note 2: In English, in addition to the common use of avenue for a wide street, avenue can also mean an approach to a problem or a place:

> The three best avenues for future research will be…

> One avenue of approach would be…

> Reading is one of the avenues to knowledge.

Side Note 3: It's a little oddity that the French word for a tree lined approach to a home has gone from a word derived from **venir**, to come *(une avenue)* to a word derived from **aller**, to go, *(une allée)*.

to ponder

The verb **to ponder** came in the late 1300's from the Old French **ponderer** meaning to weigh, to judge the weight of, or judge the worth of. Even in Old French *ponderer* was used figuratively to mean to weigh mentally, to evaluate, as well as being used literally to mean to weigh.

In Old French there were a family of words around *ponderer*, some of which were starting to be used figuratively:

> **ponderable**: *lourd, accablant* (heavy, overwhelming).

> **ponderamment:** *avec poids, pesemment, gravement* (heavily, weightily, gravely)

> **ponderant:** *pesant, qui a du poids, de l'importance* (heavy, which has weight, which has importance)

> **pondereux:** *pesant, qui pèse beaucoup* (heavy, which weighs a lot)

> **ponderosité:** *poids, pesanteur* (weightiness, heaviness)

In Modern French, *ponderamment, ponderosité* and *ponderant* have disappeared.

On the other hand, the verb **pondérer** has taken an accent and its primary meaning now is to <u>balance</u> (probably from the balancing scales that were used to weigh things), although in economics it has special uses as in "to weight" an index or an average.

The adjective **pondéreux** now means of high density (weighing a lot per cubic meter), while **pondérable** is now a technical word meaning weighable.

While these are fairly technical words, the adjective **pondéré,** by contrast, usually applies to a person and means calm, well-balanced, equilibrated. The idea of balanced may come from the verb *pondérer* (to balance).

Pondéré the most common of these words in Modern French:

> *C'est un homme pondéré* – He's very level-headed.

And there's a new noun, **pondération,** which as a literary word means equilibrium, and as a mathematical or economics word means weighting (of a variable). However, in Modern French, when a person speaks with **pondération** it means that he is calm, balanced and measured in his judgments. That is to say, he's level-headed.

In Modern English, the verb **to ponder** means to consider or weigh something carefully before deciding. It no longer refers to physical weighing, or weight. It doesn't refer to balancing, either.

The adverb **ponderable** is only used in a poetic or literary manner, and means what can be weighed, or what can be mentally weighed or considered. It's an uncommon word.

The adjective **ponderous** means unwieldy, slow and clumsy because of great weight. Figuratively it can mean labored dull and excessively solemn (overly "heavy"), as a speech or sermon.

To Sum Up: The English verb to ponder came from the French verb *pondérer* which was a member of a family of words having to do with weight, weighing, or mentally weighing. Since then, these words have each spawned a new family of words having to do with weights, balance, or mentally weighing. English has leaned toward keeping the idea of mentally weighing or weight, while in Modern French the emphasis has been on balancing or being balanced, while meanings having to do with weight tend to be technical usages.

imponderable

Now, on to **imponderable** and *impondérable*:

In French, the adjective *impondérable* dates from 1795 and can be an adjective or a noun, but in both cases the meaning is the same. The *impondérable* is what has no weight, which can't be weighed, and thus figuratively, the results of which can't be weighed in advance.

 des facteurs impondérables --- factors which

can't be evaluated in advance, imponderable factors (adjective)

les impondérables de la vie --- the things that can happen in life without explication (noun)

In English, as in French, **imponderable** is either an adjective or a noun and means difficult or impossible to estimate, to weigh in advance.

There are too many imponderables. (too many things we can't know in advance) --- (noun)

There are too many imponderable factors. --- (adjective)

For the English word imponderable to mean of very light weight or having no physical weight is only an archaic or poetic use of the word.

Interesting Side Note: The French word *impondérable* was a newly invented term in physics for things that couldn't be weighed (such as light and electricity). It started out referring to these physical things only, and it wasn't until many years later that the figurative usage was introduced.

In English as well, **imponderable** was at first a physics word applied to unweighable things, such as heat, light, electricity and magnetism, but these uses are now obsolete.

Both words originated at about the same time, at the end of the 1700's, so I can't tell you which came first. However, as they both came from *pondérable* and ponderable, which both came from the French *pondérer*, we have to say that the English word imponderable is ultimately of French origin, no matter which imponderable came first.

Historical Side Note: A few days before I was to send this book to the publisher I was reading *The Age of Innocence* by Edith Wharton, and came across the following passage:

> Archer, who seemed to be assisting at the scene in a sense of odd imponderability, as if he floated somewhere between chandelier and ceiling, wondered at nothing so much as his own share in the proceedings.

This use of imponderability sounds bizarre to our ears, but clearly in 1920, when *The Age of Innocence* was written, imponderable could have the French sense of <u>weightless</u> (and Edith Wharton obviously expected that her readers would understand it).

I checked the 1913 Webster's dictionary, and indeed, at this time the first meaning given for the adjective **imponderable** was still:

"without sensible or appreciable weight"

and imponderable was listed as coming from the French *impondérable*. The noun **an imponderable** was still only listed as a word from Physics, and referred a substance such as light, etc which was considered without weight. The word was mentioned as being no longer much used.

The figurative sense that we use now when we say "that is still an imponderable" or "there are too many imponderables," meaning that we can't judge their effects, wasn't even mentioned in the 1913 dictionary.

Reflection: It's interesting to consider how we take for granted that the word imponderable means unknowable. And yet less than a hundred years ago people took for granted that it meant physically weightless. Oh, granted that you can easily trace the path between them:

> what can't be weighed physically – what has no physical weight – what is **weightless**

> what can't be weighed physically – the results of which can't be weighed, figuratively – what is **unknowable**

That doesn't change the fact that Archer's "imponderability" meaning weightlessness sounds totally foreign to us, and that our meaning for imponderable meaning unknowable would probably have been totally foreign to Edith Wharton. How many of our words will change their meanings in a hundred years? Probably lots.

Another Interesting but off the subject Observation: If you haven't already noticed, also look at the use of "assisting" in the above passage from *The Age of Innocence*. It fits better with the sense of the French verb ***assister à*** (meaning to attend, be present at) rather than with the usual current meaning of the English verb **to assist**, which is to help or aid.

In this sentence it apparently means that Archer felt that he was in the audience, observing, as it would mean in French. This meaning is still seen in English, but it has become more uncommon.

forest

The English word **forest** came form the Old French word *forest*, which, like so many words in modern French, has lost the *"s"* and replaced it with a circumflex over the preceding vowel to form *forêt*.

chateau

You'll remember, not very far above, under **avenue**, in a quote from a 1694 dictionary, we had the following phrase: *devant la porte de son chasteau*. In Modern French, *chasteau* has made the same transformation as forest, losing the *s* and replacing it with a circumflex over the preceding vowel to form *château*.

host

The English noun **host** came from the old French noun *hoste*. You know the drill by now: *hoste* lost the *s* and replaced it with a circumflex over the *ô* to form *hôte* in Modern French, which also gives such familiar expressions as *table d'hôte* and *chambre d'hôte*.

The French word *hôte* is a bit of an oddity as it can mean either <u>host</u> or <u>guest</u>, depending on context.

hostel
hotel

From host we go to **hostel** and **hotel**. Let's look at hostel first.

In English, from the 13th to 16th centuries a **hostel** was an <u>inn</u> that provided lodging as well as food. This meaning is now obsolete and a hostel is now usually an establishment that provides inexpensive meals and lodging for a specific group of people. For example, a Youth Hostel. Here's a description from Wikipedia:

> **Hostels** provide budget oriented, sociable accommodation where guests can rent a bed, sometimes a bunk bed, in a dormitory and share a bathroom, lounge and sometimes a kitchen.

Hostel came into English in the 13th century from the Old French **hostel**. The French *hostel* had two related meanings: first, a large house or mansion (which had frequent visitors or guests), and second, an *auberge* or inn, which offered accommodations to travelers. It was also used for large often frequented public buildings and *Hostel de Ville* was listed in French dictionaries of the 1600's.

The Old French **hostel** is, of course, the Old French **hoste** meaning host, which we just discussed, with an *I* added at the end. This explains the connection to taking in guests.

In French, *hostel* lost its *s* and put an accent over the ô to become **hôtel.** *Hôtel* gradually became the preferred form of the word. *Hostel* gradually died away and disappeared. It was not listed in my French dictionaries after the end of the 1600's. *Hôtel* took its place.

In Modern French *un hôtel can be a hotel.* It can also be a large private mansion in the city. Finally *un hôtel* can be a large government building as in *Hôtel de ville* (City Hall). A private mansion is sometimes specified as *un hôtel particulier* (where *particulier* means private).

In English, on the other hand, a **hotel** doesn't mean either a private mansion or a government building. It's just a hotel.

Note that although *hostel* was replaced by *hôtel* in French, both hostel and hotel continue to exist in English. Why did that happen?

In English, **hotel** didn't evolve from hostel, of course. There was no tendency for words in English to lose an s like in French. The English **hotel** came from the French *hôtel* after *hôtel* had replaced *hostel* and thus hotel made its own separate entrance into the language. It was first used in English the 1600's for an official residence (which is now an obsolete meaning) and then as a hotel in the 1700's.

A Fascinating Side Note: But why was there room for another similar word meaning hotel in English if English already had hostel?

The answer is that the word hostel had become obsolete in English after the 1500's, even before it was obsolete in French. It was only revived a couple of hundred years later by the historical novels of Sir Walter Scott, in the beginning of the 1800's.

Thus when hotel made its arrival on the scene in English in the 17th century, the word hostel had been gone for more than a hundred years.

Something to Think About: In French, when *hostel* began to be replaced by *hôtel*, it wasn't overnight. No one flipped a switch. For a while both forms were used and the two words overlapped for decades, if not centuries, from the time the first person wrote *hôtel* until no one wrote *hostel* anymore.

hostelry

There is a whole family of words related to host, hostel and hotel. A **hostelry** is an old fashioned word for an inn for travelers. It's an ancient word related to a hostel. It came from the Old French **hostelerie** at about the same time that **hostel** came from **hostel**.

Like hostel, the word hostelery became extinct and was then revived in the 1800's.

In French, *hostelerie* and *hostellerie* were alternate spellings for the same word, both dating from the

1100's, and deriving from *hostel*. **Hostellerie** won out, and by losing its **s** and changing its **o** to an **ô** it became a **hôtellerie**.

In the old days a **hôtellerie** was a rustic inn for travelers. It was also the name for a building at an abbey that could receive guests, as abbeys and monasteries were supposed to take in travelers.

In Modern French, the word **hôtellerie** has been resuscitated and spruced up, and has become a fashionable name for a hotel or restaurant which is rustic in appearance, but which may be quite comfortable or even luxurious on the inside.

And the precursor word **hostellerie**, which had died out long ago, was revived in the 20th century. It's used the same way as *hôtellerie*.

hospice

Hospice is another word in this family of words. It entered English in the early part of the 1800's as a lodging for travelers, especially one provided by a religious order. It was only near the end of the 1800's that the word started to be used for a shelter for the terminally ill. In the 1913 Webster's, a hospice was still defined as:

> A convent or monastery which is also a place of refuge or entertainment for travelers on some difficult road or pass, as in the Alps; as, the Hospice of the Great St. Bernard.

Hospice came from the French word *hospice*. There were hospices probably since the year 1100 that were run by religious orders to shelter pilgrims and travelers as well as others that provided shelter for orphans, abandoned children, the elderly without resources, and the ill. However the <u>word</u> *hospice* in French only dates from the 1690's, coming from *hospitalité*.

When the <u>word</u> *hospice* was first used it was used for shelters for members of religious orders when traveling, or city refuges for them in times of war. It wasn't until the 1835 edition of the dictionary of the Académie française that we see *hospice* defined as a place for caring for the sick:

> Hospice: se dit plus ordinairement, aujourd'hui, de certaines maisons de charité où l'on nourrit des pauvres, des gens hors d'état de gagner leur vie, à cause de leur âge ou de leurs infirmités. *Hospice de la vieillesse. Hospice des incurables. Hospice des enfants trouvés. Etc.*

It was actually later than that when the word *hospice* began to be the word used for a place where religious orders sponsored a shelter for travelers.

In current French, **un hospice** is still used for a house where religious orders give shelter to pilgrims or travelers, but its modern meaning is as a shelter for the aged who may not have financial resources or family to care for them.

Historical Note on *hospices* and *hôpitals*. A

French dictionary of about 1875 makes it clear that the word *hospice* was being newly used as a place for the long-term ill, without resources to be kept at home, while the word *hôpital* was being used for a place of short term care, where one went to be cured of a malady.

It also pointed out that in the past the word *hôpital* had applied to all the shelters that received the poor whether they were sick or not, so that a place for short term medical care was a new use for the word *hôpital* as well:

> Hospice, Hôpital:
>
> Les hôpitaux sont particulièrement destinés à la guérison des malades ; les hospices, aux infirmes, aux vieillards, etc.
>
> L'hôpital est un asile momentané où l'on cherche la guérison d'une maladie ; l'hospice est un asile perpétuel où l'on passe toute ou une partie de son existence.
>
> Autrefois il n'y avait qu'hôpital qui s'appliquait à tous les lieux destinés à recevoir des pauvres malades ou non malades.

hospital
hospitality
hospitable
hospitably

You've probably guessed that these are from the same family of words:

hospital from the Old French *hospital* (even if it had a different meaning back then and is now spelled *hôpital*).

hospitality from *hospitalité*, etc, etc.

I'll let you take these on faith or research them yourselves. I don't want to wear out my welcome and overdo it on this huge family of words (host, hostel, hotel, hostelry, hospice, hospital, hospitality, hospitable, hospitably). They are all descended in one way or another from the same Old French root *(hoste)*.

Now, on to something different.

feast
to feast
fete
to fete

The English noun **feast** arrived from French way back in the 1200's from the Old French word *feste* meaning feast or festival. The verb **to feast** came from *fester* about one hundred years later.

As you might have figured out by now, *feste* and *fester* each lost an *s* and gained a circumflex to become *fête* and *fêter* in Modern French, but they have kept the same meaning over the years.

An interesting twist is that, some 400 to 500 years later, the transformed French words *fête* and *fêter* made independent voyages across the English Channel and were also adopted into English in about 1750 and 1820 as **a fête** and **to fête**. (The English word fête can also be spelled fete).

The noun **fête** usually means either an elaborate party or an outdoor fair. The verb **to fête** usually means to honor someone with an elaborate dinner or celebration. Here are some examples of the use of these words in English:

> The visiting dignitaries were fêted at a large reception.

> She was fêted at a special dinner.

> The opening of the show was followed by a fête for the cast and guests.

Wikipedia indicates that fête is widely used in England and Australia, where what we in the US might call a **country fair** is often called a **country fête**.

The use of **to fête** to mean to honor someone undoubtedly comes from the French *fêter quelqu'un* or *faire fête à quelqu'un*, which mean to honor someone with a feast, or welcome them warmly with a feast.

festivity
festival
festive

These are three more words from the Old French stem *feste* meaning feast.

Festivity came in the late 1300's from the French *festivité*.

Festival came about the same time from the Old French *festival*, which was an <u>adjective</u> meaning pertaining to a feast. This word later became extinct in French.

If you are wondering how *festival* could have been an adjective(!), consider the hypothetical:

> *un jour festival* --- a day with a feast, a feast day

In English, **festival** was at first naturally an <u>adjective</u> since it came from the French adjective. When it arrived in the late 1300's, it meant pertaining to a feast, then later took the associated meaning of joyful or mirthful.

Festival started being used as a <u>noun</u> in the late 1500's, with the same meaning it has today.

Both usages (adjective and noun) continued in English and both noun and adjective were listed in both the 1828 and 1913 Webster's dictionaries:

> A festival entertainment --- joyful, festive (adjective)

> I cannot woo in festival terms --- joyful, mirthful
> *Shakespeare*

> The mornings trumpets festival proclaimed ---
> celebration (noun)

Believe it or not about half my current dictionaries still list the adjective usage. Although it must be quite rarely used now, it's probably seen in older literature.

Interestingly, **festival** returned to French as an English import in the 1830's. Its primary modern use in French is for music, dance or film festivals.

Festive came from feast and from the French religious word **festif** (and **festive** for the feminine). These French words dated from the 1400's and meant pertaining to a religious feast.

The word **festive** in English came from the French in the 1600's, and at first kept the meaning of pertaining to a feast. Festive added the meaning cheerful, jolly and party-like about 1775. For example

> It was a festive atmosphere.

Festive didn't escape from its religious sense and become widespread in French until the 1970's! It still means pertaining to a feast or party.

Side Note: There are two more French words in this family which don't have English counterparts. The first is **festin** which means the meal of a *fête*, and in casual language means an excellent and sumptuous meal:

> *Merci beaucoup pour le dîner. C'était un vrai festin !* --- Thanks so much for the dinner. It was a great meal, a real feast!

The other word is **festoyer**, which used to mean to fête someone, to receive them with a *festin*, but which in Modern French means to take part in a *festin*.

premier
premiere

We'll now go to some more straightforward French imports:

The adjective **premier** in English means <u>first in importance</u>, <u>leading</u>, as in:

> one of America's premier artists (or scientists, or accordion players)

Or <u>first created</u>:

> the premier issue of the magazine

And used as a noun, in Australia or Canada a Premier (an abbreviation of Premier Minister) can be the <u>head of government</u> of a province or state.

As I'm sure you know, **premier** is French for first or chief. It's the first French ordinal number in the series first, second, third, etc. The English word **premier** came from **premier** in the 1400's.

Now on to **premiere**. In English, the noun premiere means the first performance of a piece of theatre. (It can also be spelled **première**).

> It was the Broadway premiere of his play and he eagerly awaited the reviews.

Premiere can also be used as a verb.

> Her first play will premiere on Broadway next Saturday.

> She will premiere in the play in the role of Sophie next Saturday. (It will be her first performance in the role).

> The TV show premieres at 8 PM, Sunday, August 1st.

The noun **premiere**, meaning a first performance, premiered in English in 1890. It came from the French *première*. To premiere was first recorded as a verb in English in about 1940.

In French *première* is the feminine of *premier*.

cordial

My Etymological Dictionary lists the adjective **cordial** as first arriving in English at the end of the 1300's from the Middle French *cordial*. Its original sense was of the heart or for the heart.

The noun, **a cordial**, came about the same time and referred to a medicine or drink that supposedly stimulated the heart. Now, this has evolved to mean a liqueur, which I guess was considered to be a tonic for the heart.

The <u>figurative</u> sense for the <u>adjective</u> **cordial**, meaning heartfelt or from the heart (a warm welcome, for instance), was first recorded in the 1400's. This sense of warm, friendly and sincere is the primary sense of the word at present.

Similarly, for the French adjective **cordial**, "that which would stimulate the heart" is considered obsolete or literary. As in English, **cordial** currently means what comes from the heart and is heartfelt, and refers to sentiments, feelings, a welcome, etc. The noun, **un cordial,** also has the same meaning as it does in English.

The French adverb **cordialement** (cordially) and the noun **cordialité** (cordiality), date from 1393 and 1450 respectively.

Explanatory Note: My Etymological Dictionary lists cordial as coming from the French *cordial*, and the French *cordial* coming ultimately from Latin. On the other hand, some of my English dictionaries list cordial as coming direct from the Latin *cordialis*. This is the first word I've listed where the origin seems in dispute, but in spite of the difference of opinion, I decided to give cordial a brief mention here because its origin from the word heart is so interesting, and also because I suspect that the Etymological Dictionary is correct.

The French word *cordial* dates from 1314. It's easier for me to believe that the word migrated into English from this neighboring country over the course of the century, than to believe that by a great coincidence, the <u>exact same</u> word with the <u>exact same</u> meaning just happened to be independently invented in English 70 years or so later, from Latin. It's just too much of a stretch.

carpet

The English **carpet** came from the Old French *car-pite*, originally meaning a coarse cloth that one used to cover a table, or used as a bedspread. Since then the words have gone in different directions.

In English, in the 15th century the meaning shifted to floor coverings. And in current English, a carpet is a floor covering which usually covers the entire floor and is glued or nailed down, with the exception of an oriental carpet or Persian carpet, which is a large free-standing, usually hand-woven, rug.

In French, the word *carpite* has become *une car-pette* (dating from 1863, probably passing through *carpitte* on the way, and perhaps influenced by the English word carpet). Since the 1930's at least, *une carpette* has been a small throw rug, such as you might have alongside your bed, although as recently as an 1870's French dictionary, *une carpette* was still defined a large striped cloth or *drap*.

entourage

The noun **entourage** was first attested in French in the 1770's, coming from the French verb **entourer**, to surround.

The English **entourage** is a recent addition to the language, and didn't come from the French **entourage** until the 1830's, with the meaning of surroundings or environment. It took its current meaning of the people surrounding a celebrity or important person in about the 1860's.

> The star entered, surrounded by his entourage.

It must have still been a rare word, or still considered a foreign word, in the beginning of the 20th century, as it didn't make it into the 1913 Webster's.

Intriguing but way off the subject Note: The French **entour** is a thousand year old word. In the older dictionaries it was used either a preposition or an adverb. Now the adverb and preposition no longer exist and it's a relatively little used noun meaning that which is around (something). It's usually used in the form **à l'entour** meaning _tout autour_, or _all around_ (something).

Now here's the intriguing part: **à l'entour** has been compressed by removing the accent, the apostrophe, and the space, to make the familiar French ad-verb **alentour** (which has the same meaning). And as a plural noun, **les alentours** are the environs.

This must have begun a long time ago as a phonetic transcribing of the sounds. I find *alentour* in dictionaries as far back as the 1600's and my *Petit Robert* says it dates from the 1300's.

The expression *à l'entour de* and consequently *alentour de* used to be used as prepositions, but this is obsolete, and one now says *autour de*.

to environ
environs
environment

Just above I used the word environs, and decided to look at it more closely. While investigating the words environs and environment, I also discovered the English verb **to environ,** meaning to surround or encircle. I had never heard of it and it must be a rare and very formal verb, but it is in all of my English dictionaries, so it must be legitimate:

> The old temple was environed by ruins that were not yet excavated.

The <u>verb</u> **to environ** came from the Old French **environner**, a 12th century word, which still exists in modern French with the same meaning.

> *Beaucoup de montagnes environnent la ville ---*
> Many mountains surround the city

Il s'est environné d'amis --- He surrounded himself with friends.

The <u>noun</u> **the environs**, on the other hand, is a common English word and means the surroundings. It came in the 1600's from the French **les environs**, which is also a plural word, meaning the surrounding area, *les alentours*.

Avez-vous un guide des environs de Paris ? --- Do you have a guide to the environs of Paris?

The noun, **the environment**, entered English from the French word ***environnement*** which dated from the 1300's, and also from the verb **to environ** which had already entered English.

The initial meaning of **environment** (and ***environnement*),** was from the verb to environ, and it was the state of being environed or surrounded:

the environment of the city by farmland, by floods

This meaning is now listed as rare or obsolete both in English and in French.

The environment as the total of the natural and cultural <u>conditions in which organisms live</u> was first used in English in 1827 by the British author Thomas Carlyle, who invented the meaning to translate a German word for which there was no word in English.

The <u>ecological sense</u> of environment originated in the 1950's.

Interestingly, these later two meanings made the trip

back into French in the 1960's, and are now the current meanings for *l'environnement*, listed in Le Petit Robert as *"d'après l'anglais américain* environment".

And in French environ is also an adverb used in a figurative sense and meaning about or around. For example:

> *C'est à vingt kilometres, environ* – It's at about twenty kilometres (from here).

> *Il y a environ trente membres* – There are around thirty members.

tremble

Many people probably think of the verb **to tremble** as a very "English" word. Well, **tremble** came from the Old French verb *trembler* in about 1300, with the sense of to shake from fear or cold.

The verb *trembler*, which dates from 1120, still has the same meaning in Modern French, and it can also apply to a thing as well as a person:

> *La terre tremblait* --- The earth was trembling.

> *Les vitres tremblaient sous l'effet du vent* --- The windows were trembling with the force of the wind.

Side Note: The noun, *un tremblement*, refers to a trembling itself, and *un tremblement de terre* (an earthquake) is a very common expression.

On the other hand, interestingly, the noun **un trem-**

ble is not a tremble at all, but a poplar tree, so named because its leaves seem to tremble and shimmer with the slightest breeze.

Just for fun Side Note: In looking up the verb *trembler* in older dictionaries I noticed the following from the 1st and 4th editions of the *Dictionnaire de l'Académie française* in 1694 and 1762. In successive entries you can really see French morphing into its present form:

> From 1694: *Estre agité, estre meu par de frequentes secousses.*

> From 1762: *Être agité, être mu par de fréquentes secousses.*

In this one sentence you can see *estre* lose its *s* and take on the circumflex to become *être*, and *meu* change to *mu*, part way to its present form *mû*. All just from 1694 to 1762.

hostile
hostility

This is pretty simple. The French adjective *hostile* dates from 1450. It entered English as **hostile** at the end of the 1400's. In French *hostile* still means hostile, and there are additional words *hostilement* and *hostilité* meaning hostilely and hostility, which are both actually even older than *hostile*. In fact, the noun **hostility** didn't actually arrive in English until about 1530 although the French noun *hostilité* dated from the 1300's.

(You can skip the rest of this section if you wish)
Above you've gotten the simple story. The odd part is that **hostile** practically disappeared in French during the 1600's and early part of the 1700's. The *Petit Robert* says it was a rare word during that time, although it was easy to find in the Middle French dictionary of the earlier period.

Jean Nicot in *Le Thresor de la langue francoyse* gives *hostile* just one word in 1606. It was also not listed in either the first or fourth editions of the *l'Académie française* dictionary dating from 1694 and 1762 (and therefore probably not in the second and third editions in-between either).

By the time we get to 1788, Jean-François Féraud in the *Dictionaire critique de la langue française* lists *hostile*, *hostilement* and *hostilité*, all three, but remarked that **hostile** was a fairly <u>new word</u>, and points out that the *Académie* dictionaries hadn't yet mentioned it. Here's what he wrote: *Hostile est un mot assez nouveau. L'Acad. ne l' a point mis.*

On the other hand, *hostilité* and *hostilement* were in <u>all</u> the dictionaries of the 1600's and 1700's and never fell out of use, although *hostilement* is now primarily a literary word.

It's just an interesting oddity that a word like *hostile* could fade out like that and then come back, probably coming back because the other two words were still in use (and maybe partly because hostile was in use in English).

debonair

This is an incredibly interesting word. The Old French word **debonaire** dated from the year 1080, was from the days when the nobility hunted small game with trained hawks, was a pushing together of **de bon aire**, and meant of good race. Thus, it meant thoroughbred, when applied to a hawk, or of good breeding when applied to a person.

Later, the word added an accent and a second **n** and became **débonnaire**. And somehow, (I don't know how) when applied to a person the word came to mean extremely <u>kind</u> and <u>indulgent</u>, <u>patient</u> and <u>peaceful</u>. For example here are some excerpts from the definition of *débonnaire* in the *Dictionaire critique de la langue française* of 1788:

> *Doux et bienfaisant... Les vrais Chrétiens sont débonaires... La vertu d'un grand Roi, c'est d'être débonaire. Il est, de ses Sujets, moins le Roi que le Pere.*

These meanings are now obsolete or just literary, and **in current French** *débonnaire* means almost <u>too soft</u> and <u>too mild-mannered</u>, perhaps <u>meek</u> *(bonasse)*. It's almost pejorative.

In fact, *débonnaire* came to mean so excessively indulgent and complaisant that *un mari débonnaire* came to mean a husband who tolerated his wife's infidelity.

On the other hand, **in English**, the adjective **debonair** usually refers to a man who is <u>confident</u>, <u>stylish</u> and <u>charming</u>, so the contrast between the meanings in the two languages is rather stark and takes you aback. In my book, *French Faux Amis*, I describe how I discovered this word: I was watching an American film (in France) with French subtitles. Someone was described as "meek" in the film and the person doing the subtitles translated "meek" into French as "débonnaire". As you might imagine, that really startled me.

Historically, the adjective **debonair** entered English in the late 1200's, and in Middle English meant docile and courteous (roughly coinciding with the now obsolete early French meaning).

Then, not only did this meaning become obsolete, but the word itself became obsolete, and didn't arrive again from French until about 1680, meaning pleasant and affable at that time. How debonair got to its current meaning of confident, stylish and charming may have been through the original hawking idea of excellent breeding, of good family, etc.

Actually current English dictionaries tend to give two meanings for debonair. Either suave, urbane, worldly, and charming on the one hand (of good breeding?) or relaxed, carefree, lighthearted, nonchalant, and jaunty, on the other. They may of course overlap. Gentle, friendly, and courteous is usually presented as archaic.

Interesting Note: While the "courteous and gentle" meaning is now obsolete, as recently as the beginning of the 1900's **debonair** meant mostly courteous and gentle, and the suave, urbane, James Bond sense that we take for granted wasn't even listed.

For example, here's the definition of debonair from the Century Dictionary of roughly 1914: Of gentle mien; of pleasant manners; courteous; affable; attractive; gay; light-hearted. And here's the definition from the 1913 Webster's Dictionary: Characterized by courteousness, affability, or gentleness; of good appearance and manners; graceful; complaisant. – We don't see James Bond in either of those, at all.

Personal Opinion: The transformation in English of the sense of **debonair** from "courteous and gentle" to "suave and worldly" is interesting. On the other hand, the transformation of **débonnaire** in French from "of good (noble) family" to "meek and excessively mild" is really <u>odd</u>.

nonchalant
nonchalance

The words **nonchalant** and **nonchalance** are pretty interesting as well. They come, naturally enough, from the French words **nonchalant** and **nonchalance**.

In both languages, the adjective **nonchalant** means unconcerned, unworried, indifferent and lacking enthusiasm and passion. The noun **nonchalance** is the state of being *nonchalant*, or the behavior of someone who is *nonchalant*.

These French words were built from **non** and **chalant** coming from the Old French impersonal verb **chaloir**.

Etymological Side Note: *The verb **chaloir** itself* meant to matter to, to be important to, to interest, to worry (someone), figuratively to heat someone up. *Chaloir* came from the same stem as *chaleur* and *chaud.* Thus **nonchalant** means not emotionally heated up, not acting as if the thing in question matters, is important, or is worrisome.

The verb *chaloir* is practically obsolete and currently is used only in the expressions:

> *Peu me chaut --- Peu me importe.* It matters little to me.

> *Il ne m'en chaut --- Il ne m'importe.* It doesn't matter to me.

Even these expressions are now rare in current French.

It was interesting to follow the demise of the verb *chaloir. Le Thresor de la langue francoyse* of 1606 gave 36 (!) sentences illustrating the use of *chaloir.* However, by 1694, the dictionary of *l'Académie* française gave just two examples and said *Il est vieux* (It's an old word). The 1762 edition of the same dictionary said that it was pretty much only used in the expression *Il ne m'en chaut,* meaning *Il ne m'importe.* Thus from 1606 to 1762 it went from being a widely used verb to a practically extinct one.

In any case, *chaloir* gave birth to *nonchalant* and *nonchalance,* which are still very active words in both languages.

mizzen mast

This is a sailing word, and I can't claim to know anything about sailing, but I did discover accidentally that it comes from French. (You'll have to excuse any errors I make about sailing, but what I say about the word itself will be correct).

I ran across the word when, in a seaside resort and port, I passed a bar and café called *Le mât de misaine*. When I sounded it out I realized that it was The Mizzen Mast.

The English word **mizzen** came from the French *misaine* in the early 15th century. While *misaine* comes from an Italian word meaning middle, in French it has moved forward on the boat. It appears that currently *la misaine* is *la voile basse du mât de l'avant du navire (autrefois du milieu),* and **le mât de misaine** is *le premier mât vertical à l'avant du navire.*

On the other hand, In English, the mizzen mast has moved toward the rear of the boat. It is the mast closest to the stern in a ship with two or three masts. It's just aft of the main mast, which makes it the third mast if there is also a foremast.

Side Note: The French word *mât* came from the Frankish word *mast*, with the usual change of losing the "s" and adding an accent on the vowel before.

elegance
elegant

These are pretty straightforward, coming at the end of the 1400's from the French *élégance* and *élégant*.

In French, the noun *élégance* refers to an esthetic sense of <u>harmoniousness, grace and simplicity</u>. It can refer to form, or to a fashion of speech.

> *Il s'exprime (ou il écrit) avec élégance* --- He expresses himself (or writes) elegantly.

It also refers to <u>good taste</u> in dressing, in manners and behavior, and in fashion.

> *Elle s'habille avec élégance* --- She dresses with the best of taste (it doesn't mean elaborately and richly as it might in English).

> *J'aime l'élégance de cette preuve* --- I like the simple beauty, the elegance of that proof.

> *Il sait comment perdre avec élégance* --- He accepts defeat well / with elegance.

In English, **elegance** has the same meaning, but picked up a second meaning of refined luxury or tasteful opulence, in about 1800.

The French adjective *élégant* refers to things or people who have *élégance*, that are in good taste, graceful and stylish (or in science: ingenious, pleasing and simple).

une femme élégante, un style élégant, and even, by extension, *un restaurant élégant.*

In English, **elegant** has the same meaning, but can also refer to things that are luxurious and opulent while keeping good taste.

an elegant woman, an elegant solution to the problem, an elegant party

a paraphrase
to paraphrase

The noun **a paraphrase** means a restatement of what someone else has said or written using different words, often in an attempt to state things more clearly. It came into English in the 1540's from the French word *paraphrase*, which itself dated from the 1520's.

Here's a quote from *Le Thresor de la langue francoyse* from 1606:

Paraphrase, *C'est à dire Exposition et interpretation qui ne se fait point de mot pour mot* --- Paraphrase, That's to say Exposition and interpretation which isn't word for word.

The French verb form *paraphraser* dates from 1535, but apparently **to paraphrase** wasn't used as a verb in English until about 1600.

a sentence
to sentence

The simpleminded story about sentence is that sentence means about the same thing in English and French in a legal sense, but that in grammar, the French word for a sentence is *une phrase*.

However, as you'll see, there's a lot more to it than that. A lot! And it's a lot more interesting as well!

The French noun **une sentence** dates from the 1100's. In Old French it had two different meanings.

One was the legal sense which it still has today. In French, **la sentence** is the <u>decision</u> of a judge or of an arbitrator. It's similar in English, but not quite the same, as **a sentence** usually means the <u>punishment</u> handed down. For example:

He received a sentence of twenty years.

The other Old French meaning for **une sentence** is now fairly outdated or obsolete in Modern French. This the idea of a memorable saying or thought, especially on a subject which touched on morality, which could be referred to as a <u>maxim</u>, an <u>adage</u>, an <u>aphorism</u> or a <u>precept</u> of moral behavior.

You may wonder how the same French word came to have two such different meanings. Well, the meaning of the word started with the idea of "sense" or "good sense", and then evolved into meaning or significance, then to an opinion, and finally to a judgment.

The idea of a maxim came from meaning and significance, while a judge's decision came from the idea of an opinion or judgment.

Sentence entered English from French with this second meaning of <u>good sense</u>, <u>meaning</u>, <u>significance</u> or <u>thoughts with meaning or significance</u>. This has of course become obsolete but here are some examples from as recently as Webster's 1913 dictionary:

> "Tales of best **sentence** and most solace."
> *Chaucer* - (He possibly meant "good sense")

> "The discourse itself, voluble enough, and full of **sentence**." *Milton* - (He seems to have meant either authoritative teaching or good sense).

An adage or maxim was also listed as a meaning for a sentence in English (as well as in French) in 1913, but is now obsolete.

Sentence didn't pick up the meaning of a <u>decision</u>, and then a <u>punishment imposed by a court</u> until later. Here from the same dictionary is an example of the use of sentence to mean a decision (but not a court issued judgment):

> "My **sentence** is for open war." *Milton.*

The verb **to sentence,** meaning <u>to pass judgment</u> in a legal sense, began to be used about a hundred years after the noun began to be used for a legal judgment.

And the idea of **a sentence** as a <u>grammatically complete statement</u> evolved from the idea of something which made sense and had meaning by about the middle of the 1400's. By this time, the evolution of the word sentence in English had separated from that of the word *sentence* in French, and the word for a grammatically complete statement in French is **une phrase**.

a bottle

The All-American word **bottle** came from the Old French **boteille** in the mid 1300's. It originally referred to a leather wine bottle or wineskin. The modern French word has added a letter and is now **une bouteille**.

cachet

In English, **cachet** usually means prestige, but it can also mean distinction or refer to a special mark or seal, for instance that placed on envelopes for some special event, or to an official seal of approval.

Those appear to be somewhat unrelated meanings, which we have often found to mean that there is a story involved.

Well, the original meaning of the French word **un cachet** dated from about 1460 and referred to the hard (usually metallic) stamp with which someone (the king, for example) would use to put his imprint on wax after he had used the wax to seal a letter or other document.

By extension, starting perhaps a hundred years later, **un cachet** became a general word for <u>any stamp</u>, such as was used by a bottler on his bottles of wine, or by a business to <u>distinguish</u> its product, and eventually, by the <u>post office</u> to cancel a postage stamp. It was also, by extension, used for a seal indicating <u>approval</u> by some governing body. For example

le cachet d'une marque commerciale

le cachet d'un fabricant

le cachet de la poste

By the 1760's, **un cachet** had also started being used with a <u>figurative</u> meaning, to indicate something with a <u>special distinction</u>. Here are a few examples of this kind of use from modern French:

Le château donne du cachet à ce village --- The chateau gives some distinction / prestige / cachet to this village.

Ça lui donne un certain cachet --- That gives her a certain distinction. That gives her a specialness.

The first recorded use of cachet in English was a borrowing of *cachet* from the French to refer to a seal affixed to a letter or a document. This was in 1630, but the usage must have been fairly rare and sporadic as cachet didn't make it into the 1828 Webster's (although it was in the 1913 Webster's).

Historical Note: From about 1625 until the French

Revolution, *une lettre de cachet* became infamous as a letter under the king's seal by which a person could be imprisoned without trial or explanation.

Unrelated Note: In pharmacy, dating from the late 1800's, the word *cachet* has also been used to designate a sort of capsule in which a presumably bad tasting medicine is placed in a benign tasting shell to facilitate swallowing.

to flirt

When I described the book I was writing to a French friend, she suggested I should include **to flirt**, which she said came from the old French expression ***conter fleurette*** which got expressed phonetically, and then came back into French as an *anglicisme* as *flirt.*

I decided to see what I could find out and it turned out to be quite a tangled web. Here's what I discovered:

Flirt used to be spelled flert or flurt and is thought to have come from the Old French ***fleureter*** which came from the word *fleur* (or flower). The verb ***fleureter*** literally meant to move from flower to flower like a bee, and figuratively meant to just touch lightly or brush by. It's easy to see how a bee's bouncing from flower to flower could be likened to flirting.

The diminutive ***fleurette*** was a 12th century word, which came from *fleur*, and naturally meant little flower. In the early 1600's it took the figurative sense of gallant remarks and ***conter fleurette à une***

femme meant "to whisper sweet nothings" to her, to court her.

By the time of the first edition of the dictionary of *l'Académie française* in 1694, the word **fleurette** was hardly used any more to mean little flower except in pastoral poetry, but was primarily used figuratively. Here's a quote from the dictionary (excuse the outdated spelling):

> *Il signifie fig. Cajeolerie que l'on dit à une femme: Dire des fleurettes, conter des fleurettes. elle aime les fleurettes.*

The excellent Dictionnaire de la langue française from 1872-77 by Émile Littré gave a couple of interesting etymological discussions. Here's the first:

> *Fleurette, diminutif de fleur...C'est par une métaphore facile à saisir que des propos galants ont été assimilés à une petite et jolie fleur. Il y avait un verbe fleureter, qui signifiait babiller, dire des riens.*

> (*Fleurette*, diminutive of flower... It's by a metaphor which is easy to grasp that gallant remarks have been compared to a pretty little flower. There was a verb *fleureter*, which meant to say little nothings).

And here's a second:

> *On nomme flouretas, fleurettes, de petits compliments d'amour dont les fleurs sont à la fois le prétexte et les termes de comparaison. L'usage*

en est très ancien dans notre Midi. (and gives an example dating back to 1484).

(The little compliments of love for which flowers are both the occasion for, and the terms of comparison, are called *fleurettes*. Their usage is very ancient in our South of France).

The noun **un flirt** and the verb **flirter** then came back into French in the middle of the 1800's as *anglicismes* and they are still used today.

Flirter is used in the same way as to flirt in English, but *un flirt* isn't used quite in the same way as a flirt is used in English. As I pointed out in *French Faux Amis*, *un flirt* isn't a flirtatious person but a brief romantic relationship, more than a flirtation, maybe more like a fling:

> *Elle a eu un flirt avec Jean. C'était son premier flirt* --- She had a brief romantic relationship with Jean. It was her first romance.

On the other hand, flirtation and flirtatious didn't make it into French and you can't use them in French.

Historical Note and Discussion: (You can skip this if you're impatient, but it's interesting).

To flirt has had other senses in English. One, which is now rather rare, that of making a quick somewhat jerky movements, as in: she flirted her fan, or the bird flirted its tail.

Flirt, with the meaning to move in short quick flights,

to move in a <u>darting motion</u>, or to move inconstantly from <u>object to object</u> was noted as far back as the late 1500's and undoubtedly came from *fleureter* and its bees.

To flirt could also mean to <u>fling suddenly</u>, as in: the boys flirted water at each other.

There was apparently another word to flirt which meant to <u>jeer or sneer at, to mock</u>. This seems to have been a totally unrelated word and is now obsolete.

In a separate development, the noun a flirt was used for a "pert <u>young hussy</u>" or a woman of loose behavior.

All of these senses for flirt were still in the 1913 Webster's, along with the current meaning.

Thus, while some of the words we have covered in this book are self-evident (niche <u>is</u> *niche*, after all, and ruse <u>is</u> *ruse*), **flirt**, as I mentioned before is a more tangled web. **Let's try to untangle it:**

1. To flirt, as we commonly use it today, clearly originated with the figurative use of the noun **une fleurette** (a little flower) as a little <u>compliment</u>, given to a woman while <u>courting</u>.

2. The meanings of quick <u>short movements</u>, quick <u>short flights</u>, and <u>darting</u> movements probably all evolved by extension from the verb **fleureter** which referred to bees going from flower to flower.

3. Moving <u>inconstantly</u> from object to object also came from the same source. The dictionary of Old French gives examples of the use of the figurative sense of <u>barely touching on</u>, even back then: *Nous avons seulement fleureté sur la doctrine;* and also of the use of the figurative sense of <u>skipping from thing to thing</u>: *Je me suis mis à fleureter.*

4. We can imagine the idea of a <u>loose woman</u> coming from that lack of constancy. From there, we can see the development of the English noun, **a flirt**, which if you think about it has a different and somewhat more pejorative meaning than the relatively harmless verb, **to flirt**.

5. To flirt in the sense of to <u>jeer</u> or <u>sneer</u> at, or to <u>mock</u> was probably another word with the same or similar spelling. It doesn't seem to have any connection with any of the other senses we've discussed.

laissez-faire

You really had to work on that last word, so here's a straightforward one. The French expression *laissez-faire* has been taken directly into English as **laissez-faire.**

As a noun, **laissez-faire** means a policy of letting things take their course without interference. It's usually used in politics or in economics, and can be an adjective as in laissez-faire capitalism (in which governments let the free market determine how things will turn out without regulation or interference).

It came from the French economic expression **lais-sez-faire**, literally "let people do" (as they think best), in 1825.

a rash

I never would have thought of the noun rash as a French word, but it is believed to have come from the obsolete French word **rache**, from the Old French **rasch** or **rasche**, meaning eruptive sores, or ring-worm sores.

In the 1872-77 *Dictionnaire de la langue française*, **rache** was already listed as a word of *autrefois* (in other words, obsolete) even then.

> *rache: nom sous lequel on désignait autrefois les diverses maladies éruptives de la tête, et, en particulier, la teigne* (ringworm).

The current French word for a rash would be *une éruption* or *une rougeur*.

A rash is sometimes used <u>figuratively</u> in English for any sudden proliferation or outbreak. This usage dates from the 1820's.

> There has been a recent rash of break-ins in our part of town.

escarpment

In English, an **escarpment** is a long steep slope

or precipice, especially at the edge of a plateau, or between two different levels of land surface. It's a word used in geography, geology, and especially in mountain climbing and hiking.

However an **escarpment** was also used as a military word, especially in the days of fortresses, and described land which had been transformed into a steep slope on the exterior of a fortification to make it more difficult for attackers.

Naturally enough, **escarpment** came from the French word **escarpement** (with an extra **e**) in the 1820's. The French escarpement dated from 1700 and was part of a family of words. This included:

> **escarpe**, dating from about 1550 and again being the steep embankment of a dry moat used as part of a fortification.

> **escarper**, meaning to make into a steep slope, now extinct except for the past participle escarpé. The verb escarper hasn't been extinct long, however, as I found it listed as recently as in an 1872 French dictionary.

> **escarpé** which is used as an adjective, meaning made into an escarpement, steep. And finally,

> **escarpement** itself, which meant, as with the English escarpment, a steep slope or cliff. A rare secondary meaning is the state of being steep (l'escarpement de la côte).

Note: While **une escarpe** (fem.) is an embankment,

un escarpe (masc.) is a completely different word coming from old French slang meaning a professional robber or assassin. Similarly, **un escarpin** is a fine woman's shoe, and comes from a different family of words, eventually from an old Italian word meaning shoe.

bouillon

The English word **bouillon** (usually pronounced approximately "bul-yon") is a usually clear broth made by stewing meat, fish or vegetables in water, and saving the fluid afterwards.

Bouillon came in the 1600's from the French word which is also spelled **bouillon** but is pronounced roughly "buwee-yon". **Bouillon** is an old word from the 11th century, and comes from the verb **bouillir**, to boil.

Le bouillon can refer either to the bubbles of air which form when a liquid is boiling, or as in English, to a liquid in which certain foods have been boiled.

calm
the calm
to calm

The English **calm** came from the French *calme*, and the two words still have almost identical meanings.

Further Etymology: In French, *calme* was first the noun **le calme** in the early 1400's from the Italian *calma*, which meant calm but also referred to the time of day when nothing moves because of the heat of the mid day sun. The Italian *calma* itself came from the Latin *cauma* (also meaning heat of the midday sun), from the Greek *kauma*, also meaning heat, especially of the sun.

By extension, the French **calme** came to refer to the condition of the wind and sea being calm (presumably in the heat of the day), and was generalized from that to the state of the absence of things happening. In English, the figurative application of calm to a societal or political condition, or to a state of emotional calmness, came in the 1500's.

Returning to French, the French **calme** as an adjective came about 150 years after the noun was first used, that is in the 1550's, from the noun *calme*.

The verb **calmer**, to calm, came from the adjective *calme* and meant at first to diminish a feeling or sensation *(calmer une douleur, calmer la soif, calmer votre colère)*, and afterwards took the meaning to relax someone or something *(Elle essaie de calmer l'enfant)*.

The reflexive **se calmer** means to calm oneself. For example:

> *Calme-toi !* --- Calm yourself down! (Mother to child)

> *Le bébé s'est calmé* --- The baby calmed down.

The odd little maritime verb **calmir** is a variation of *se calmer*, meaning to become calm. For example:

Enfin, la mer (or *le vent*) *calmit.*

Finally the adverb **calmement** means calmly.

As you can see, all three of the noun, adjective, and verb (as well as all their meanings), have made it into English.

tranquil
tranquility
to tranquilize

While we are on calm, we can touch briefly on tranquil and tranquility. **Tranquil** came about 1600 from the French word *tranquille* which dated from the middle 1400's.

Tranquility is even older, being adopted into English in the late 1300's from the French *tranquilite* (now *tranquillité*).

In French, the verb *tranquilliser*, to calm or make tranquil dates from the 1400's.

Cette idée me tranquillise --- That idea calms me.

The English verb **to tranquilize** came two centuries later.

On the other hand, **tranquilizer** as a sedative, and as a member of a family of anti-anxiety medications, developed in English first, from the verb tranquilize, and returned to French in 1960 as *tranquillisant*, as an English import.

liaison

The English noun **liaison** has a number of different meanings. It can mean a close working relationship involving cooperation, often between or within an organization.

> He works in close liaison with the New York office.

A liaison can also be the person who works in liaison:

> He is our liaison with the New York office.

In a different sense **a liaison** can be a sexual relationship, which often involves secrecy and may or may not involve infidelity:

> They've had a liaison for several years now.

In phonetics **liaison** refers to the sounding of a final consonant that is normally silent before the initial vowel sound of the next word. For example, les amis (pronounced "lay zami").

Finally, in cooking, **the liaison** is the binding or thickening agent of a sauce, often based on egg yokes.

Note that all of these meanings for **liaison**, disparate as they seem, involve the <u>binding or tying together</u> of things or people.

This word, **liaison**, came from the French word *liaison* in the middle 1600's. The French word *liaison* itself is a very old word, dating from about 1200, and it comes from the even older French verb *lier*, which means to bind, to tie, to link up, to thicken (in cooking), to fasten.

In French, **liaison** generally means a connection, link or bond. It can be used to refer to ideas:

> *Ses idées sont sans liaison* --- His ideas don't hold together.

Or a communications link:

> *liaison par satellite / liaison téléphonique* --- satellite link / telephone link

Between people *une liaison* can be a romantic affair, but usually *être en liaison avec quelqu'un* means to be in touch with someone, and if you say *deux services sont en étroite liaison* that means that the two departments are in close liaison, just as in English.

Liaison is also used in transportation to refer to connections between two cities or two places.

In linguistics and in cooking *liaison* has the same meaning as liaison has in English. In brick masonry *liaison* is the bonding, mortar or cement. In chemistry *liaison* is a bond.

Liaison first arrived in English as a cooking word which was just a minor application of the French word **liaison**. It afterwards took the more general meaning of a connection, link or bond between people or things from the French word.

Other words in the word family in French include:

liaisonner, a construction word, meaning to bond or to grout bricks together.

lier, the original verb, meaning to bind, to connect, to tie together

liant, as an adjective: quick to make friends, to connect to other people

un liant, as a noun, a technical word meaning binding agent.

un lien, a tie, a bond: *les liens du mariage / liens de famille / liens d'amitié.*

crime
criminal

These are pretty simple. The English word **crime** came in the 13th century from the Old French *crimne*, which in modern French is *crime*. The original meaning of *crimne*, which is not surprising for the 13th century, was sinfulness. It later came to mean crime, which it still means today.

The English word **criminal** came two centuries later from the French *criminel*, an even older French word than *crimne*. Both criminal and *criminel* can be either nouns or adjectives.

Side Note: *Crime* and *criminel* have developed a large family of associated words in French in the same way that crime and criminal have done so in English. These include, for example: *criminalité,* *criminaliser, criminologie, criminologue, criminaliste, criminalistique, etc.*

forfeit

The English word **forfeit** is another word which was originally a "crime" word, but which has a couple of interesting twists.

The noun **a forfeit** came from the French ***un forfait*** or ***forfet*** (a crime or transgression) in about the year 1300.

This French noun ***forfait*** was originally the past participle of the verb ***forfaire***, which is now obsolete or just literary, but which meant to transgress the laws, to act contrary to one's duty, or contrary to how one should act.

The meaning of a **forfeit** started out in English to mean a crime. The etymological dictionaries say that the sense shifted in English in the middle of the 15th century from the crime to the penalty, but my *Petit Robert* gives what may be a better explanation. They list another meaning for ***forfaire*** from the feudal legal system as follows:

> *Forfaire un fief pour cause de félonie*, le rendre confiscable par quelque forfait --- To forfeit *(forfaire)* an estate held on condition of feudal servitude because of a crime, make it able to be confiscated because of the crime.

In current French, ***un forfait*** is a heinous crime (as

distinguished from a normal crime). It's a literary word but not an obsolete word at all.

And *un forfait* never means a forfeit. Except in horseracing that is, where the *anglicisme* **forfait** was imported to mean a fine or forfeit paid for scratching a horse (withdrawing him from the race) at the last minute. And by a figurative extension, it spread to other sports even where there was no money forfeited:

> *L'équipe à déclaré forfait* --- The team forfeited the match (withdrew).

Note that the French word **fortaiture** doesn't mean **forfeiture**.

> As a feudal word, **fortaiture** meant breaking ones pledge of homage, and thus was treason.

> As a literary word **fortaiture** means a lack of loyalty.

> And as a legal word **fortaiture** is a crime in which a public figure (governmental) commits a breach of trust while carrying out his or her duties.

In all three cases the **fortaiture** is the crime and not the punishment.

Important Side Note: There's a second word **forfait** which you'll hear much more frequently as it's a much more common word, and which apparently came from a different source. This **forfait** is a commercial word and refers to a fixed price package. For example:

J'ai un forfait de trente euros par mois --- I have a fixed price of thirty euros per month (for telephone and internet service, for example)

un forfait de ski trois montagnes --- a three-mountain ski pass (for a fixed price).

Elle a eu un forfait-vacances --- She had a holiday package.

Historical Notes: It was between the 4th edition of the dictionary of l'Académie française in 1762, and the 5th edition in 1798 that the definition of **forfait** changed from just *crime* to *crime énorme, atroce*.

By the 1st edition of this dictionary in 1694, the commercial sense of **forfait** had already been listed: *un marché, par lequel un homme s'oblige de faire une chose pour un certain prix, à perte ou à gain* (an agreement by which a man commits himself to do something for a certain price, whether he ends up making a profit or not).

Summary: We clearly need a summary here, as this has been rather complicated.

Okay, **in French**, the verb **forfaire** meant to transgress the law or not live up to one's duty. The noun **forfait** came from *forfaire* and meant a crime. Currently it's become a literary word and means an atrocious crime. There's another unrelated noun **forfait**, used in current speech, which is a commercial word and means a fixed price package.

In English, a forfeit came from the French *forfait*, and thus used to mean a crime, but now is what you lose as a penalty for committing a crime. The verb to forfeit means to lose property or freedom as a penalty for committing a crime or as a penalty for other wrongdoing or for neglect or for abandonment (He forfeited his deposit by not showing up).

The meaning of forfeit may have changed spontaneously from the crime to the penalty, but it is more plausible that it came from an alternate meaning of the French *forfaire* in feudal law.

Finally, the English forfeit was imported back into French as *un forfait* in horse racing and other sporting events, etc.

basin

The Old French word *bacin*, meaning a receptacle for water, dated from the 11th century. It entered English as basin in the 13th century.

Basin has since taken several geographic meanings in addition to meaning a receptacle: a natural depression on the earth's surface, containing water, dates from the 1700's, and a river basin, or area drained by a river, dates from the 1800's. It can also mean a sheltered area where boats can be docked, as in a yacht basin. You'll note that all of these keep the general sense of a receptacle for water.

The Old French *bacin* has changed to *bassin* in

modern French. It can be used for the same geo-graphical features as the English basin, and in addition can be used for an ornamental pond or pool in a garden:

> *les bassins du Luxembourg* --- the ponds in the Luxembourg Garden in Paris

You are also likely to hear *le bassin* in a medical context as it also means the pelvis.

There is an associated word *une bassine*, which instead of being a diminutive, means a larger and deeper receptacle for cooking or industrial use, larger and less portable than an ordinary household *bassin*.

> *une bassine à frites* --- a large pot for making French fries

basil

Basil, the aromatic herb used in cooking, came hundreds of years ago from the Old French *basile*, which is now *basilic*.

barrette

This word for a bar shaped woman's hair clip or hair ornament came from the French *barrette* in the early 20th century. It is a diminutive of the French word *barre* which means bar or rod.

Barrette is the kind of word which is obviously French, if you stop to think about it, because of its *ette* ending. However, if you're like me you've never really thought about it.

to deign
to disdain
disdain

I had never thought of **deign** and **disdain** as related words, probably because of the different spelling. But they are related, very related.

The English verb **to deign** came from the Old French *deigner, deignier,* or *degnier*. The original meaning of to deign was to consider something worthy or fit. It has currently changed to also mean to condescend to do something that you think is beneath your dignity.

You may, at first glance, think that these are entirely different meanings, but consider how deign is used:

He didn't deign to answer my question.

With the modern meaning you'd translate this as:

He didn't condescend to answer my question (as he felt it was beneath his dignity).

but, you could also use the original meaning to translate it and you wouldn't be far off:

He didn't think it was worthy or fit to answer my question.

He didn't think my question was worthy of an answer.

Note Deign is usually (but not always) used in the negative. For example: "He didn't deign to" or "He wouldn't deign to". And it's often used in sentences which are ironic and pejorative towards the person who is not deigning, with the implication that he or she is a snob or feels very superior.

Here's a couple of examples of deign that aren't in the negative. They are still ironic though with an implied accusation of snobbishness in them:

She deigned to visit Margaret when she was sick at home.

She deigned to eat at my humble abode.

While in English deign has kept close to the original spelling, in French the spelling has changed to *daigner*.

Daigner can be used in the sense of to condescend, as in English:

Elle a daigné me rendre visite.

Il n'a pas daigné répondre.

"Je supplie votre majesté de daigner lire avec attention cet ouvrage" (Voltaire).

It can also be used ironically or sarcastically as in:

Daignerais-tu fermer la porte? --- Would you please close the door!

Now on to the verb **to disdain**. To disdain came from the Old French ***desdeignier***, from the earlier *desdegne* or *dedeyne*, about a century after the verb deign entered the language.

The French *desdeigner* came, of course, from **des** (to do the opposite of) and **deignier** (to think worthy, to treat as worthy). It meant to consider unworthy, to scorn, to disdain, etc.

In modern French *desdeigner* has changed to **dédaigner**, following **daigner**. However, to disdain and *dédaigner* have retained the same meaning.

Note: As the sources of deign and disdain are *deignier* and *desdeignier*, you can see why I started this section saying that these two words are very related.

There is also a <u>noun</u> **disdain**, denoting the feeling that something (or somebody) is not worthy, in other words, a feeling of scorn. The use of the word sometimes (but not always) implies that the person exhibiting disdain is being a bit arrogant, is putting on airs, is snobbish, etc.

> He looked around at the people in the room with disdain.

The English noun **disdain** came from the Old French noun **desdeign**, which came from the verb *desdeigner*. The noun **desdeign** later changed to *desdaign* or *desdaing*, and to the current French **dédain**.

Il a répondu avec dédain --- He responded with disdain.

Je n'ai que du dédain pour lui --- I have nothing but disdain for him.

faux pas
faux

These are pretty clear-cut. *Un faux pas* is literally a false step in French. In English and in French a **faux pas** means a social blunder, an error in etiquette, a tactless remark or act, an embarrassing mistake, by either remark or behavior, in a social situation. It was first imported from French into English in the late 1600's.

Oh! She really committed a faux pas last night when she asked about their daughter's pregnancy.

I used the wrong fork? Oh! What a faux pas! (ironic)

Interestingly, *faux* itself, which means false in French, has come to be used in English, attached to English words, to indicate that something is false, fake, not genuine, imitation, or synthetic. For example:

I lost my necklace but it was just faux pearls.

The counter is just faux marble but it's very attractive.

It's faux fur.

In recent years, **faux** has even been used by itself, with French pronunciation, to mean false.

clothing words

Time for some clothing words. Since France has so influenced clothing fashions for such a long time it's natural that many of our clothing words come from French. Since there are quite a few of these clothing words, I'll try to zip through them fairly quickly.

chemise

In current English, a **chemise** is a woman's loose-fitting undergarment or long nightshirt or nightdress, usually of attractive material like silk or satin with a lace trim. It can also be a style of woman's dress, loose and straight-hanging from the shoulders.

Chemise came from the Old French *chemise*, meaning an undergarment or a garment worn under a tunic. In modern French *une chemise* is technically a man's shirt while *un chemisier* is usually a woman's blouse, but *une chemise* can actually be a shirt for either sex.

The long loose-fitting nightdress is called a *chemise de nuit* in French.

pants

The English word **pants** is a 19th century abbreviation of **pantaloons**, itself a 17th century import from French *pantalon* which referred to a one-piece total body set of tights, running from neck to feet. It came from the name of a character in Italian comedy who wore tights to cover his scrawny legs.

In modern French **un pantalon** is a pair of pants or trousers.

robe

A robe comes from the Old French **robe** meaning a long, loose outer garment.

In modern French, while **une robe** still means a long, loose outer garment when talking about a judge's robe, a priest's robe, or a *robe de chambre*, etc, the most common use you'll encounter for *une robe* is a woman's dress.

In English, a robe never means a woman's dress.

Irrelevant but Interesting Etymologic Side Note: *Robe* entered Old French from Old German with the original meaning of booty from pillaging, of which clothing was an important part. It's thus related to the same stem as rob and robbery.

blouse

In English, a **blouse** is a woman's garment resembling a shirt, opening in the front with buttons, and usually with a collar and sleeves. Blouse is a "new" word in English, arriving in the 1830's from the French **blouse**, which at that time meant a belted, loose, peasant or wagon-driver's shirt.

Historical Note: *Une blouse* first had the meaning which I mentioned above in the 1798 dictionary of the *Académie française*. Before that *les blouses* were the holes in the corners of a billiard or pool table, a word from the late 1600's. In modern French, *blouse* still has this billiard table meaning, as well as meaning an overshirt that you might wear over your other clothes to protect them *(une blouse de peintre, d'infirmière).* Its <u>primary</u> meaning though is a loose woman's shirt, as in English.

brassiere or bra

"Wait a minute!", you say, the French word for brassiere is *un soutien-gorge.* But hear me out.

The English word **brassiere** came in the 1700's from the French **brassière**, a tightly fitted woman's upper undergarment. This word is now obsolete, and in modern French *une brassière* is a infants short blouse-type outfit.

Finally, *une brassière de sauvetage* is a life vest.

Side Note: *La gorge* means the neck or throat in French, but as a literary euphemism it is also used for the breasts or bosom of a woman. Thus we have the word *soutien-gorge,* a word from the late Victorian era which didn't offend anyone's sensibilities by mentioning *seins* (breasts). As another example of the euphemism of using *gorge* for breast, a robin "redbreast" in English is called a *rouge-gorge* in French.

to maintain

The *soutenir* of *soutien-gorge* comes from *sous* (under) and *tenir* (to hold) and thus is to support (from below). We'll now go to another interesting word built from *tenir* with the addition of a prefix.

The English verb to **maintain** naturally comes from the French **maintenir**, with the same meaning. The word **maintenir** was built from **main** (hand) and **tenir** (to hold), and thus "to hold in the hand", and from that to conserve in the same state (from the 12th century). The idea of **maintaining** a <u>verbal</u> position by stating it and affirming it with perseverance dated from about 1300 in French.

To maintain arrived in English from the French in the 1200's. Its sense of affirming a position in speech began in the mid-1300's.

Mayday

"Mayday?" you ask. "Isn't that a holiday or something?"

Well May Day is a "holiday or something", but **Mayday** is the international emergency distress signal for boats or airplanes in trouble. It's believed to be a phonetic transcription of **m'aider** and short for **Venez m'aider!**

Mayday can be either an adjective or a noun:

I hope someone is within radio range. I've been sending out Maydays for a half hour already and no response yet! (used as a noun)

It's pretty faint, but I think I'm picking up a Mayday signal! (used as an adjective)

the drapes
to drape
drapery
couturier
mannequin

The family of words dealing with drapes came from the 12th century French word ***drap***, which was a kind of (woolen) cloth. From this came the verb ***draper*** a century later, which meant to make or fabricate this cloth *(le drap)*. ***Un drapier*** or ***une drapière*** was a person who made and sold *drap* or *draps*.

Let's continue with *une draperie* which had two meanings. First, ***une draperie*** could be a factory of *drap,* or a store selling *drap*. Second, ***une draperie*** could be a piece of cloth or clothing made of *drap*.

It wasn't until the 1670's that ***draperie*** began to mean cloth or clothing hanging in loose folds, at the same time that the verb ***draper*** started to be used in the same way, meaning to drape a figure in loose (and harmonious) folds.

Now let's look at the English words which came from them. The word **drapery** came from the second meaning of *draperie*, and started out meaning cloth. It only started meaning cloth with which something is draped in the 1680's, coming from the French word which had taken this meaning shortly before.

The English verb **to drape** came from the verb *draper* and naturally enough started off meaning to weave or make cloth. It wasn't until the mid 1800's that it started to be used for draping cloth, arranging it loosely or casually around something.

The American word **drapes**, meanng curtains, evolved in English from the verb drape and from the noun drapery. There is no French equivalent word *drapes*. It doesn't exist. The French word for curtain is *rideau*. If you are using **drapes** to mean hangings, the best French translation is *tentures.* While it is possible to use *draperie* for either *rideau* or *tentures, tentures* are usually made of heavier material than *rideaux.*

Side Note: In current French, this is still a big family. The most common meaning you'll hear for **un drap** is a bed sheet. (Regionally, in Belgium, it can mean a towel). The compound word **un drap-housse** is a form-fitted bottom sheet. The verb *draper* when used in textiles still means to process wool, but in ordinary speech it means to drape. **Une draperie** is still a cloth factory. In the Fine Arts, *draperie* can mean drapery. Finally, *draperie* can also be used for *tentures* or *rideaux* (hangings or curtains). The noun *le drapé* is the *ensemble* of folds in a cloth in a dress, the hang of a dress. Another noun, *le* *drapement* is the action of draping material and its result. The French word *drapeau*, meaning flag, is, of course, part of the same family.

Il faut changer les <u>draps</u> --- It's necessary to change the sheets.

Mets le <u>drap-housse</u> d'abord --- Put on the undersheet first.

Le couturier a décidé de <u>draper</u> une étoffe sur le mannequin --- The couturier decided to drape a piece of cloth on the mannequin.

Note that both **couturier** and **mannequin** came from French (in the 19th and 18th centuries respectively).

To continue:

Les jolies ondulations des <u>draperies</u> de la fenêtre --- The pretty folds of the hangings at the window, of the curtains.

Cette robe a un beau drapé --- That dress has a beautiful way of hanging.

Tu as réussi. J'aime bien ce drapement --- You did well. I really like the way that cloth hangs / lies.

drab

The adjective **drab** also came from the French *drap* in the late 1600's meaning having the <u>dull brownish color</u> of natural, undyed cloth. **Drab** expanded its meaning to the figurative sense of <u>dull and lacking interest</u> in the 1880's.

Side Note: This drab is apparently not related to another English word drab which refers to a slovenly woman or prostitute. This latter word preexisted the drab meaning having a dull color, and came from Low German or Dutch *drabbe* or *drab*.

chisel
scissors

The other day my wife asked me what the French word was for a chisel. My dictionary said it was *ciseau*, but I knew *ciseaux* were scissors. That led me to more do a little more investigation. It turns out that *ciseau* in the singular means **chisel**, but *ciseaux* in the plural are **scissors**.

The English word **chisel** came from the Old French *cisel* (now *ciseau)* in the 14th century.

The English word **scissors** came later in the 14th century (as **sisoures**) from the Old French *cisoires* (now *ciseaux)*. Note that scissors and *ciseaux* are both plural words.

Side Note: There is quite a family of French words built around these two words. The Old French *cisel* is still present in:

the verb *ciseler*, to chisel

the art of *ciselure*, working with a chisel in jewelry making or engraving, or chasing, for instance

the nouns *cisèlement* or *ciselage*, the act of working with a chisel, or of cutting off bad grapes off the vine in winemaking

when it is spelled *cisellement* it seems to refer to chasing or engraving

the person noun *ciseleur* or *ciseleuse*, is the artisan working with the chisel.

On the other hand *cisailles* are big shears, wire cutters, hedge clippers, etc.

the verb *cisailler* means to prune branches, shear metal, or cut yourself

and *cisaillement* is the cutting or shearing of metal or the pruning of branches.

Finally, *cisoires*, the precursor word for scissors, still exists, as a specialized very large metal cutter used by boilermakers, but it's a rare and technical word.

an essay
to essay
an assay
to assay

The English word **essay** has a number of different meanings.

First we have a rather uncommon literary and formal verb, **to essay**, meaning to make an initial attempt or endeavor, especially a tentative attempt at something, to try it. It can also mean to subject something to a test, although I haven't heard it used in this way.

> They've decided to essay a reform of the welfare system.

> We're going to essay a visit to my prospective mother-in-law.

To essay can very rarely mean to test the composition and purity of metals but this is usually spelled **to assay**. In fact assay and essay tend to overlap a bit.

The verb to essay has a companion noun, **an essay**, which means an initial attempt, a try or an endeavor, again especially a tentative one. This, also, is an uncommon word from more formal or literary language.

> It's just a first step towards reform, an essay. We'll have to see how it goes.

In a special case, an essay is what they call a trial design of a postage stamp, which has not yet been formally decided on.

Finally, **an essay** is a short piece of writing or composition, usually on a single subject, and usually presenting the author's point of view.

While the meanings of essay in terms or attempts or tries, which I discussed above, are uncommon if not rare usages, **an essay** in the sense of a written composition is a <u>very common and current</u> English word.

> I had to write an essay on my favorite films for my composition class.

> The admissions application includes a short essay by the student on why he or she wishes to attend the college.

Let's look at the origin of these words. For the noun and verb essay meaning an attempt or try, the origin is fairly obvious. The French verb **essayer** is the standard French word for to attempt, to try, to test, to put something to the test. The noun **un essai** means an attempt, or a try.

Essayer dates back to the 11th century and came into Anglo-French in the late 1300's with the spelling **assayer** or **assaier**, and the noun *un essai* arrived as **un assai**, primarily with the sense of putting something to the test (a metal, for instance). This spelling has remained in the words **to assay** and **an assay**.

The alternate spellings **an essay** and **to essay** entered English in the late 1400's, again from the French verb **essayer** and noun **un essai.** They arrived with pretty much the first two senses we mentioned above, to try and a try.

So far, that seems easy. So where did **an essay as a short composition** come from? And there's the story! Here's the short version:

Michel Eyquem de Montaigne was a French *seigneur*, of the Renaissance Era. In 1571, at the age of 38, he retired to the tower of his chateau near Bordeaux, where he had his library, to reflect on life. There, in near isolation, over the next ten years, he wrote a series of reflections on life which he called *essais*, or "attempts", to understand himself, humanity, and the world. The *Essais* or **Essays of Montaigne** became famous throughout Europe and influenced many subsequent writers and philosophers, and essays have been called essays ever since.

The longer version follows:

Historical Note: Montaigne came from an interesting family. His grandfather had become very wealthy as a herring merchant (!) and bought the estate (presumably from an impoverished nobleman), in 1477. Montaigne's father had been a soldier in Italy for a while and had been mayor of Bordeaux. Montaigne's mother, on the other hand, came from a wealthy Sephardic Spanish Jewish family.

Michel was born in 1533 and his father had planned out an unusual humanist education and upbringing for him. His first three years were spent in a small cottage on the estate with a peasant family so that he would feel "close to the common people". He was then brought back to the castle where his entire upbringing from age three to six was in Latin, so that he would be fluent in that language. His intellectual education (in Latin) was under the care of a German tutor. He was also taught Greek using the same method, which employed games, conversations and meditations. A musician playing a zither was assigned to accompany him from the moment he awakened, to play whenever he was unoccupied. He was not obliged to do anything but was given all the tools to enable him to profit from his freedom.

At the age of six, he was sent to the most prestigious boarding school in Bordeaux, then under the direction of a great Latin scholar of the time. He completed the entire curriculum by age 13 and went on to study law in Toulouse. He became a prominent attorney and by the age of 24, in 1557 he was appointed a counselor at the high court *(parlement)* in Bordeaux. It was at this time that he became close friends with the humanist poet Étienne de la Boétie. He spent two years also as a courtier in the Court of Charles IX. He married at 33 and had six daughters, of whom only one lived past childhood.

He started writing his *Essais* in 1571 at the age of 38. His essays are humanistic and filled with skepticism, and with tolerance for human foibles. They are an attempt to understand himself and his own nature foremost, as well as human nature and mankind in general. He especially emphasized that our knowledge is imperfect at best, and that we have an obligation to be kind to other human beings as well as to animals and to nature.

Montaigne constantly reworked his essays, even after his ten years of isolation. He was twice elected mayor of Bordeaux in the 1580's, and died at 59 in his chateau while working on a final edition of his *Essais*. This last edition was published after his death.

Postscript

For you, Dear Reader, who if you have followed me thus far must be, like Michel de Montaigne, a searcher after knowledge, this seems a fitting place to finish this volume. I hoped that you found it as fascinating as I did.

A list of my sources and an alphabetized list of the words covered in this book follows.

Sources and References

I used the following reference books to supplement my knowledge from everyday reading and conversation in the preparation of this book. They are presented in no particular order, but I do try to say a word about what I found useful in each. If I have omitted any reference, it was inadvertent and I am truly sorry, as I wished to present this list as an aid for those who wish to pursue their own researches.

The New Oxford American Dictionary (2005), which is built into my Mac OS X operating system, is excellent for definitions and also has very useful brief etymological references.

The Merriam-Webster Online Dictionary is based on the Merriam-Webster's Collegiate® Dictionary, 11th Edition (updated annually). This also is useful for definitions and has helpful brief etymological references. (http://www.merriam-webster.com/)

The Online Etymologic Dictionary (2010 and constantly updated). This is an incredibly useful source for etymological information. (http://www.etymonline.com/)

Harper Collins French Concise Dictionary, 2nd Edition, Harper Collins, (2000). This is my everyday, always in use, French-English Dictionary.

Harrap's Shorter Dictionnaire, Anglais-Français Français-Anglais, 7th Edition, Chambers Harrap, (2004). This is probably the best there is for a comprehensive English-French dictionary. It usually doesn't have etymological references.

Webster's New World Dictionary, Second College Edition, Simon and Schuster, (1982). An excellent dictionary and sources for what was used in English over a generation ago. Also has some etymological references.

Le Petit Robert, Dictionnaire Alphabétique et Analogique de la Langue Française, Dictionnaires Le Robert, (1993). Very comprehensive French dictionary which has useful etymological references, as well.

Le Petit Larousse, Grand Format, Larousse, (2001). Not as comprehensive as the Petit Robert, and without the etymological references, but useful for definitions.

Dictionnaires d'Autrefois, The ARTFL Project at the University of Chicago, online, allows you to reference French dictionaries of the 17th, 18th, 19th and 20th centuries. http://artfl-project.uchicago.edu/node/17. Incredibly useful. Includes, in chronological order:

Jean Nicot's *Thresor de la langue française* (1606)

Dictionnaire de L'Académie française 1st edition (1694)

Dictionnaire de L'Académie française 4th edition
(1762)

Jean-François Féraud's *Dictionaire critique de la langue française* (1787-1788)

Dictionnaire de L'Académie française 5th edition
(1798)

Dictionnaire de L'Académie française 6th edition
(1835)

Émile Littré's *Dictionnaire de la langue française*
(1872-1877)

Dictionnaire de L'Académie française 8th edition
(1932-5)

Webster's Revised Unabridged Dictionary (1913 and 1828 editions!) also sponsored by the ARTFL Project at the University of Chicago. Very useful to get an idea what English was like in the early 1800's and 1900's. This is online:
http://machaut.uchicago.edu/websters

The Century Dictionary Online (1914). This is a lot more complicated to use as you currently have to download a plug-in to view it, but it's interesting once you get past that obstacle.
http://www.global-language.com/CENTURY/

Lexilogus Dictionnaire français en ligne. This online site not only gives you access to a French dictionary, but to over a dozen past dictionaries, dictionaries of synonyms and antonyms, dictionaries of terms, etc.

I especially found the **ancien français (Old French) dictionary** incredibly interesting. It was compiled in 1880 to 1895 as a dictionary of French from the 9th to 15th centuries (!). I found that I could read Old French much, much more easily than I could read Old English. Old French has odd and idiosyncratic spellings, but if you sound it out you can usually figure out what they are saying, but the Old English had a lot of pre-Norman Conquest words that have no relation to anything you'd recognize. Don't miss this site. lexilogos.com /francais_langue_dictionnaires.htm

Online (French) Etymological Dictionary of the CNRTL (Centre National de Ressources Textuelles et Lexicales). I used this one a little less often, but it was useful as well. http://www.cnrtl.fr/etymologie/

Wikipedia has been very, very useful on a number of occasions when I was researching the origins of words. http://www.wikipedia.org/

Wordnik.com was also a very useful site, giving access to a number of different dictionaries for comparison. http://www.wordnik.com

Alphabetical Listing

pistol	52	splendor	35
ponder	64	tranquil	111
potpourri	60	tranquility	111
premier	81	tranquilize	111
premiere	81	tremble	88
rash	107	veracity	4
rifle	56	verification	4
robe	125	verify	4
ruse	11	veritable	4
scissors	131	verity	4
sentence	98	very	2
serge	26